AF378893

Mini and Micro-cars
Yesterday...Today...and Tomorrow

Mini and Micro-cars
Yesterday...Today...and Tomorrow

Written and Illustrated by
John Tow Shanton

Wasteland Press
Shelbyville, KY USA
www.wastelandpress.net

Mini and Micro-Cars:
Yesterday...Today...and Tomorrow
by John Tow Shanton

Copyright © 2006 John Tow Shanton
ALL RIGHTS RESERVED

Third Printing – February 2009
ISBN: 978-1-60047-067-7
Cover designed by John Tow Shanton

NO PART OF THIS BOOK MAY BE REPRODUCED IN ANY
FORM, BY PHOTOCOPYING OR BY ANY ELECTRONIC OR
MECHANICAL MEANS, INCLUDING INFORMATION STORAGE
OR RETRIEVAL SYSTEMS, WITHOUT PERMISSION IN
WRITING FROM THE COPYRIGHT OWNER/AUTHOR

Printed in the U.S.A.

*Dedicated to my father
...he taught me to drive sensibly...by example*

TABLE OF CONTENT

CHAPTER ONE

Talking About Cars...

When you got a hold of this book, I am sure the first question that came to your mind was: "Hmmmmm..., mini and micro-cars, what in the world are they?" You searched for the table of contents, but you found none. Looking puzzled, you decided to check the book out anyway, and so you flipped through these pages, and you knew why: Too many cars to list in this rambling rigmarole of a car show guidebook! And—the many interesting charts.... With a shrug of the shoulders, you decided to not put it down. That was when you found yourself suddenly teleported through a star gate into the infield of a very special car show—our mini and micro-car show of shows!

You are in—and you are a VIP!

Walking past the cars parked on the paddock, you see quite a few you never knew existed. A number of them will strike you as standing a bit awkward. Some are so outlandish that you do a double-take. You move on, not bothering to take a closer look at them. But there are many that will get you excited and wanting to open them up. They are that cute!

1

You amble on, and come up to a little bubble of a car an Isle of Man company in the UK built in the sixties. You are totally intrigued by it. Its engine is tiny. Just 98cc. You think "moped," but your mind recalls the world famous Isle of Man Tourist Trophy races, and all at once, the powerful roar of a hundred racing motorcycles overwhelms you. But you have an interesting little car to check out, and so you snap out of your reverie and go on to read about its superb gas mileage. 100 MPG! Wow! Amazed, you walk on, and then, you see me—your tour guide.

Yes, I am here to show you around—with the help of this fully illustrated book. We will have lots of fun with it, for it is not something heavy to lug around, like some dull and ditch-watery historical recounting of all things mini and micro-automotive. It is our little show companion. One thing it does have is plenty of info. And I hope interesting enough for you to share with your friends.

Often, we will be time-traveling, so hold on to your hat. But rest assured that you will not be in for a bumpy ride. With me by your side, our car talk will be more fun than anything. That despite the fact that you may find me rather opinionated. Why, I am one who still believes that cars are the stuff of dreams. I grew up in the era when they were flashy, and may I be so bold to add—sexy. Sleek and yet shapely in all the right places, they took your breath away.

Well, look at them today. Many cars are getting to look more like buses and trucks—so tall and tippy they are. I can fill a whole page about how lacking in balance and design harmony— many of the latest cars. Several chunky ones even have the stance of muscle-bound midgets on steroid. If you were to study their "faces" you could see some go "ga-ga," with their gaping grilles, others look confused and cross-eyed, or even a little anguished and constipated. It makes one wonder what their designers and stylists were thinking. Or smoking. Could it be that they have run out of ideas? Was that the reason why one prominent carmaker went chasing after a bunch of sophomores for some? Honda's "patchwork" Element is proof positive that college kids have few clues as to what constitutes good style. It seems anything on wheels that can accommodate a mattress would get the thumbs up from them. Then, of course, a luggage compartment with a deep well built in—specifically designed to hold several bags of ice and a couple kegs of beer will get their high fives every time. The new Scion xB ("B" is for "Breadbox," I suppose.) which Toyota is aiming at the younger set is another case in point. Think of the amount of fuel it will need to chug-a-lug, just to keep up with the rest of the traffic.

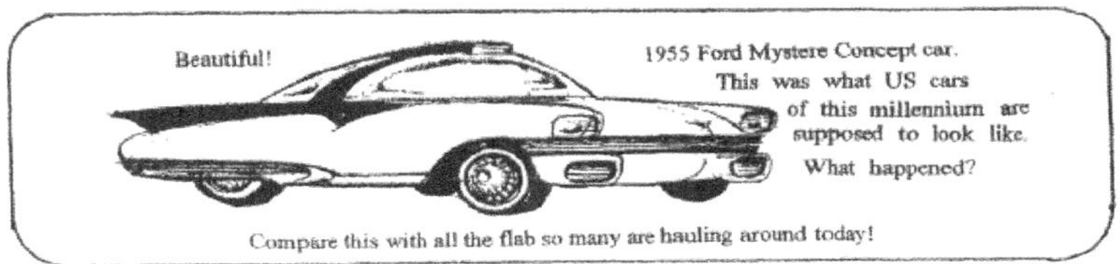

Thus, it would be well for all carmakers to steer clear of these types of design roadblocks. I remember how very taken up I was by pictures of GM's dream cars—even as a kid. They were terrific. That so few of them ever made it into production could be why the company is hitting the speed bumps today. I bet if they took a page out of their concept car picture book and did something with it, everybody would sit up and take note.

Ford too, should go back to when their Mystere dream car was shown. It was a sensation in the mid-fifties. Now, just think how exciting it would be for a car like that—with a little nip and tuck here and there, to show up in our auto dealerships next year! Here is a 100% American car. A standout. Not at all a slavish set-in-stone design dead-end the Brits call "pedigree."

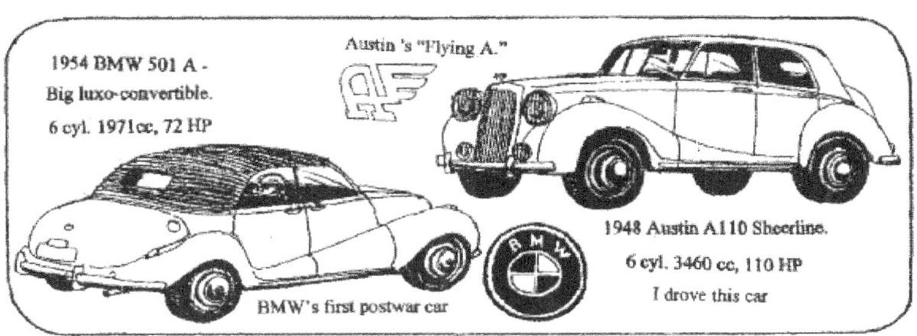

Talking about British cars, large and small, I say, many of the oldies had the finest lines. Some of their larger cars were absolutely classy. Take the Austin Sheerlines, the Bentleys, and the top of the line Jaguars. The curvaceous Marks 9s and 10s were better styled in my opinion than the Rolls Royces. Notice how graceful their fender-lines. Among the smaller cars, we still see in the area old car shows—the AC Aces, MG-TFs, Morris Minors and the antique Morgan Plus 4s remain perennial crowd-pleasers. I can go on and on... If I were to include the hundreds of classics that hail from the European continent, I would need to host a whole new show.

Still, I will never forget the time when I saw how untidy this eighties Jaguar XJ Sovereign's "trunk lid—taillight tango" was. I could not have missed it for a mile, even as the stealthy Jag sliced through traffic and swiftly got away. The squiggly way the taillight was cut up to fit the trunk lid told me that its designer must not have been on speaking terms with the folks in the car's tail-end committee. That Jaguar Cars is by no means into any copycat work is plain to us. But how did such a conflicted tail-end design get passed by the panel overseeing their work?

Cars do not get stamped out overnight. From concept to completion, any one model could take many years of hard work by teams of highly paid specialists. The product gets planned, and then, the plans are implemented with the expenditure of millions of developmental dollars, not to mention the logging of billions of man-hours of work. The talented people who form the core design group are usually hand-picked. Between each phase of progress, committees meet long hours to brainstorm and to address the hitches as they come up. Often, they burn the midnight oil. Until success is assured, the pace will go on, and with increasing tempo as the dateline approaches.

Yet, I have seen finished products that score very low in the area of appeal. So low that they assault my eyes when I look at them. It is like the cars got designed in 2-D—with just a set of French curves and a straight edge. Without the benefit of full-scale clay modeling to get things right. So, the woes a walk-around can uncover. Take a bead, if you will, at any of today's cars with a "modernized bull-nose" from the rear three-quarter view especially and you will see how ugly it is. Go check out the PT Cruiser. Compare its lines with cars of the forties and you will know why retro-half-measure-rehashes always equal ungainly. Yet, they are going ahead with a convertible version of it. Talk about making a silk purse out of a sow's ear. Therefore, every time I see car stylists get carried away with trying to hodge-podge the old and new, I know that they have run out of ideas. Even the latest Ford Mustang tells me that. Take a quick look at this 2005 retro-pony car. It could be mistaken for a well-kept sixties' model at a glance! Likewise, so poorly packaged are a great many cars out there today that I cannot but wonder how they managed to make it all the way to the production line—past the seven or eight figures representing the amount of money earmarked for their creation.

Let me list a few examples of the little foxes that spoil the vines, even from the driver's seat, so you know my drift: make-believe glove boxes that are not wide enough to hold, of all things, a regular-size road map; door pockets that are just too skimpy, instrument panels that scream info overload; control knobs with labels utterly lacking in logic, cup holders that are too tricked up for safe use; tons of cheap chrome-plated trim on the instrument panel that glare at you on a bright sunny day; dash-tops so styled that you cannot put anything on them; fancy white-faced dials galore that distract you to no end. And I have not even begun to get out for a walk-around for a little "grille-talk," or a peek under the hood. Well, later.

That cars today are regarded by many as "appliances" could be why they are no longer the stuff of dreams. Take your pick of the makes and models currently stamped out by automakers everywhere, and you will be hard put to tell them apart from fifty paces. So pervasive is the culture of copycats among the scores of marques out there! It is no wonder that many of us have lost our first love for the automobile. For why, are they not morphing more and more into something as nondescript as a blob with every passing year? It does look to me that the trend is to build them ever bigger and heavier. But I know there are many who do not want to be muscling these chunky looking delivery vans around every live-long day. For every "buy big" car shopper there has to be a "buy small" one, I am sure of it.

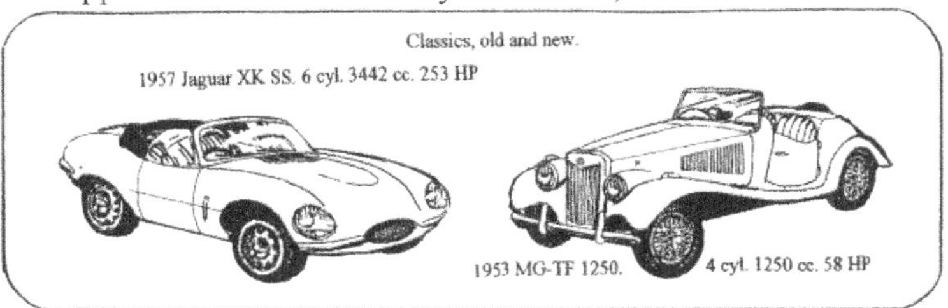

Now, I am not implying that there is no place for big cars. Larger vehicles are truly a godsend to many moms with kids, not to mention the "soccer moms" who depend so much on them to bus their broods around. Without the extra room they would not be able to haul things like gym-bags, backpacks, band-instruments and other what-have-yous, plus their teens, tweens and in-betweens, together with the rest of the Brady Bunch, to where they have to go. And that, mind you, after they have made their rounds with their rug-rats, while all loaded down with diaper bags, strollers, and all to their breakfast clubs.

For sure, there is a whole group of people in our society that needs more than just a car to get about. Therefore, I cannot discount the importance of SUVs and trucks. We have people looking for both the large and small vehicles. Being in the trades, I have often thought about buying a pickup myself. With that said, let us press on.

Even so, I will have to say that many of the "just a car," of today, meaning the regular three-box, two-or-four-door kind, have become too much car for most of us. Ask yourself how many unrepentant piston-heads among us are left who will gleefully open the hood and peek around in there when something does not sound right. If the fancy Chinese-puzzle of an engine cover is not off-putting enough, try sorting out the rat's nest of plumbing and wires in there. Our carmakers have made the cars of today no longer owner serviceable. In other words, "user-friendly." Why, they know there is gold to be got for every turn of the wrench. Look at how much they are charging for the scheduled maintenance alone. To not void the warranty, you may have to let their shops look at your car at points along its many mileposts and pay them a ton of money to do so. I say, therefore, to be honest, every one of these factory mandated charges should be factored into the actual cost of the car.

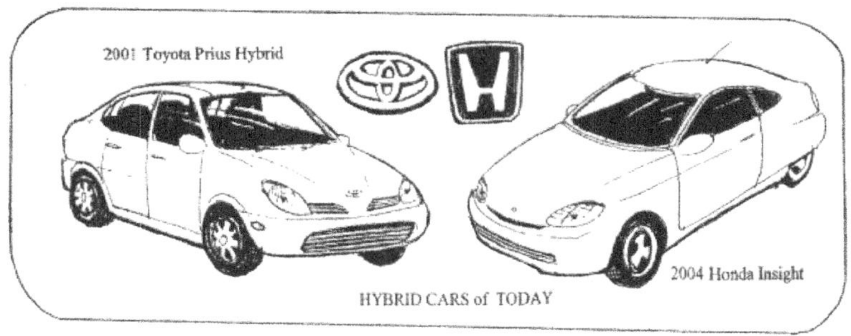

Now, don't get me wrong, there are still many cars made today that are beautiful, though each in its own way. Looks has always been a matter of subjective opinion. Everybody is allowed to cast a vote, and every vote, however biased, counts in that department. All the same, with many "entry level" models out there costing upwards of ten-grand, there will be a great company of people who will not be able to afford to buy a new car. Indeed, in this day and age, most of the cars that are real super are beyond just about everybody's reach. Especially the over-engineered and needlessly loaded ones with power operated everything, not to mention the spacey up-to-the-minute models with the new hybrid drives. The lauded true gas-savers. Or, "gas saviors." But the part about how the scheduled maintenance costs alone, of a hybrid could drive one to the poorhouse is seldom mentioned, for obvious reasons.

The latest magazines showing off the 2006s are in the newsstands now. Check them out and you will see that most of the new cars listed do not seem to be doing any better on gas compared with last year's offerings. The average MPG is about 20. It's absolutely appalling! Shouldn't the numbers get better every year? And shouldn't our cars be times more trouble-free too? I often wonder why Detroit is not putting out more and more cars that can squeeze a ton of miles out of every gallon of gas. They have direct connection to OPEC, and so, they must be years ahead of any of us when it comes to the question of oil price and supply. With whole departments staffed by well-paid hirelings dedicated to plumbing the depths here and in the Mid-East, they should be. That is, if they have not already turned each mahogany row and ivory tower into one big country club.

It is a shame that good gas mileage is no longer the selling point for most of our cars. Of all the 2005's, there is only one car I would qualify as an "econocar." The Toyota Echo. It is both low in cost, and easy on gas. But we all know that this car was given just about the most tepid kind of reception by the automotive press. Could it be why 2005 will be the last year Toyota will be making it? Come to think of it, the very word that denotes gas-efficiency has taken on a meaning that is quite negative in our country. Just try calling a car that takes little gas to run an "econobox" today. If it is not regarded a "penalty-box" put-down by our status-stupid society, what is? Ah, how well has Detroit brain-washed us all into thinking that going small is somehow silly. Even insane.

Therefore, the little public outcry about the price of gas at the pumps today. As a result, our automakers are going their merry ways, cranking out the heavier, gas-guzzling autos like there is no tomorrow. They know that a nation used to being wasteful will never really care even if gas went up by twice as much. Just make more of it available! So steeped are we in our "bigger is better" mindset that we will pay whatever the cost to sit tall in the saddle.

You may think that I am all down on big cars. But that is not the case, for I am fully subscribed to our need of the larger automobiles. To my mind, the Big Three should go on building their big profit behemoths and all the humongous what-have-yous among us. But they should not forget to include the smaller cars on their to-do lists. And in this new millennium, they should most certainly be getting ready to tool up for the micros too.

The cars at the small end of the scale may not be the big money makers as they do not have many "empty calories" to push, but they will pay real dividends down the road, when the times get leaner, and meaner. Even if things do not get bad, I say build them and let the marketplace decide. I know that many of the wiser ones in our affluent society will eventually find it practical to substitute their second or third car for something small and fuel-efficient should the times get tougher. Who is to say that many others will not be weighing their options in a similar fashion, and be going with what is best?

Did not BMW's wise decision to build the Isetta "rolling egg" save them from going belly-up in the fifties? Their bold and contrary-wise move put them out in the forefront of the automotive world. It showed the public how quick on the canvas this great old German carmaker could be when the going got tough. It was able to target both ends of the model spectrum and score good hits. Imagine a manufacturer of deluxe limos putting out a people's micro-car. By doing so, it gave a whole generation of everyday drivers a chance to try out a premier marque's product, and to see what good is. Why? BMW not only settled down to turn out the licensebuilt Isetta as per Iso's blueprints, but it also improved on it. So, when their big and buxom gas-guzzling 501s were not selling during the years right after the Second World War, their thrifty egg-shaped 300s, kept rolling out the door and kept them from getting swallowed up by Mercedes Benz.

I say, therefore, putting more smaller cars in production today will in like manner, keep our nation from being shackled by the oil sheiks and help us break free of our addiction to oil. At least it would get us headed in that direction. Just one little gas sipper for every ten super-sized cars sold, let's say, would do it. Within a few years' time, all the gook and gunk of "big is better and bigger is best" would begin to get cleaned out of our system, and it would not be long before we will never want to go back to our old fuelish ways again. Even Detroit will get degreased and go clean and green, building cars for a whole new generation where conservation of our resources by going small and preservation of the environment by thinking green will be big.

Ah, perhaps there are even as we speak, some car company reps from the Big Three, milling around incognito among the crowds, looking to get some ideas from the little cars featured here?

Here are cars, lots of them smaller than small, that were at one time very popular because they did not cost much money to buy, register or operate. A great number of them have over the years taken on celebrity status. As they become more and more appreciated their practicability will soon be apparent. Indeed, there are many clubs all over the world today, literally hundreds of them, actively meeting to celebrate, restore and show these thrifty little cars off. I counted over

200 of them, just in this Dutch classic car annual that I am using for my research. Imagine this many car clubs in tiny Holland! If you were to check out the clubs in your state, I am sure you will find not a few yourself. All having fun with their little gems while they work to keep them humming. However plain their choice of make, they command such devotion! I have been to some of the meets, and I tell you, I have met so many seemingly ordinary people there who are truly the most resourceful of engineers,—the way they are able to bring any old rusted hulk on wheels back from the bone yard! Yes, these tiny old cars, some with the barest of basics have given so much pleasure to millions today.

Today, gas prices have soared again. Our European cousins the Dutch are already paying over $6.00 a gallon to drive. We used to pay just 99 cents not too long ago. Now we fork out three bills, and the end is no where in sight.

Still, many here consider the price increase to be a mere inconvenience. A non-issue for those with cash and flash. Basically, it is—if you have got it, flaunt it! Life is too short, so live it up. Go big. Be a hog, that is! How well have the clueless been conditioned by Detroit's horsepower hype to keep their blinkers on.

Ah, the countless numbers fueling up with fifty-dollar bills now and commuting to work in their heavy haulers with nary a shrug of their shoulders.

In the latest USA-Today newspaper, I read an article talking about how Detroit is trying to "tweak" (actual word used) the MPG numbers of their big gas hogs to make them sell better in this tight oil market. You know our carmakers are beginning to feel the heat. The sales of their larger cars have taken a nose-dive of late, and so, they are doing whatever it takes to turn things around. How? GM announced that they have eliminated the radio whip antenna from their huge Tahoe SUVs. By so doing, they are hoping to increase its gas mileage by 0.001 MPG. Well, I say that is stupid! One quick goose of the gas pedal, and many times the 0.00 1 MPG saved would be blown out the tail pipe. There are other more effective measures that they could take.

Being an avid student of auto body design, I am persuaded that drafting a good, wind-cheating envelope for the Tahoe would be the easiest way to go. The air is much like a fluid, and as it has "body" it can be hard to "swim" through. Smoothening all the parts that stick out would help too. As would the elimination of the roof-rack.

Do their design staff know how the frontal area of a car, van or truck can affect is fuel consumption? Simply put, the bigger the grille, the greater the guzzle. Look at how super-sized, many of the car and truck grilles in their current line-up. Totally vulgar. It is no wonder that some after-market parts manufacturers have begun to poke innocent fun at Detroit, making these outrageous looking toothy bolt-on fangs for the really gaping grille-works, to make them look more like rampaging T-Rexes going: "R-o-a-r-r-r-r!"

Instead of getting serious about addressing the real problems—the escalating (Doesn't that call to mind "Escalade" as in Caddy? What a name for an SUV for such a time as this!) crisis Big Oil is drowning our nation in, and the wholesale trashing of our environment by the reckless and irresponsible among us, our experts are humoring us with these silly little sideshows. Should they not be doing whatever it takes, to engineer a way to cut down on fuel use?

In Holland, there is on the road, a tiny four-wheeled vehicle called the Virgo Range. This most forward of nations has taken the lead in many areas of modern society, and I am sure, what goes there will eventually filter down to ours. They have bravely gone where no man has gone before, in many things, and who is to say that we will not be following in their steps one day. So, could the Range, or cars like it, now in rather wide use there be also our chosen mode of transportation here in the not-too-distant future?

A write-up about this car says that it "costs next to nothing to run, is effortlessly green, easy to park, and thread through city traffic, and is so simple that reliability is usually assured." A bold statement! My folks there sent me a photo of it, parked next to their Mazda Protégé and its smallness was immediately evident. Yet, it did not look flimsy at all. More pictures of it and other micro-cars that are currently in production in Europe can be found in the last several pages of this book. But before we fast forward to them, let us time-travel back to the fifties and take a look at the forerunners of this little car.

Virgo Range micro-car

To set the stage, picture yourself in Europe just after World War Two. Much of it had been reduced to rubble. With the defeat of Hitler's war machines, all of Germany's manufacturing capabilities were zilch and rationing was the order of the day. I know that in Holland, for example, bread, the staff of life, stayed on the list till the fifties! Everyone was pulling tight and working hard to salvage what little was left of their homeland. As in all civilized and mechanized societies, the masses clamored for a truly economical way of getting about to expedite the process of rebuilding and to help them get on with their lives. The postwar cars that were eventually put out were like what they had made before the war—the large fancy cars that were not only expensive but also unsuitable for the harsh times. For example, the ordinary man in the street could not afford luxo-limos like the BMW 501. (See page 3) Money was tight. Even with the normalization of relationships between the former warring parties, much needed help was often not forthcoming.

So, enterprising engineers, or really, "imagineers,"- sat up, took note of the people's requests and began to draft up plans to manufacture small, cheap-to-run one or two-cylinder powered automobiles to fill the need. The plan was to make do with what little they had. They succeeded, for their venture put Europe back on wheels during that very difficult period of their history. Thus, many car historians today, reviewing how those little cars that were mass-produced in the fifties helped get all of Europe rolling, refer to the desperate decade after the war to be the Golden Age of the micro-cars.

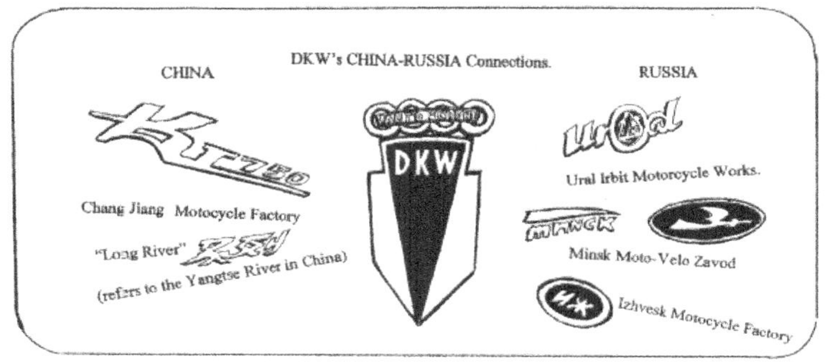

As the right material were either rationed or in short supply, many of the carmakers had to innovate in order to facilitate things. One pots and pans manufacturer turned automaker cut up his surplus aluminum cookpots to make the fenders of his cars. Picture a half-a-cook-pot car! More later. Many of the results were therefore rather crude even by their standards in the early years. But progress was nevertheless made by all.

The engines used to provide motive power, however, were already well-tested, being supplied by their many big-named motorcycle factories. Take DKW. Its KT-125 two-stroke design was so trusty that its blueprints were included as a part of Germany's war reparations. BSA, Yamaha, and Harley Davidson were all awarded them. So, the many in the motorcycle world who have come to love the indomitable BSA Bantams, and to know about Yamaha's YA-1 beginnings. Perhaps you too, have heard about the small but sweet-running Harley Model 125 Hummers which were built between 1946 and 1965?

I should mention too, that Russia's ubiquitous IZH-350s (Izhevsk) produced by the legendary Ural Irbit Motorcycle Works were also DKW copies, as were the Vostoks and Moskva M1As made by Minsk Moto-Velo Zavod of Belarus. The Cossacks 650Ds, also made by Ural Irbit were however, from a BMW design, and their Mars M-63 combined the best of BMW R-66 and R-75. And would you know too, that BMW's unstoppable R-71 was what inspired Harley Davidson's wartime XA army bikes? Shaft-driven, it could muck around where no ordinary chain-driven bike could. It was the war-bike the German Wehrmacht took to the deserts of North Africa, and the forever cold tundras of the Eastern Front. We have been told that this very same venerable motorcycle design and engine are still being produced in Russia and China today! For about US$5,000, you could buy a Chinese version—the Chang Jiang 750. It is a clone of the IZH M-72, a tough Russian bike that incorporates the best qualities of BMW's R-71 and 75. Really, it is not too many bucks for a true classic, considering what they are asking for an ordinary Harley, German Beemer, or Japanese rice rocket in the showrooms today. There is a Ural dealership right near here—in Red Lion, PA, of all places, if you are interested. Check out Adamson's Susquehanna Cycle, 890 W. Broadway, or look up his website at www.adamsonsuscycle.com. Parts should not be a problem too, for Ural Irbit Motorcycle Works have recently established a manufacturing plant in Redmond, Washington. That is great, good news for the many in our midst who would like to ride, or collect these rugged, no-nonsense, totally time-tested, machines.

What can I say but this—we got the rocket scientists after Germany surrendered but the Soviets and the Chinese got Germany's best motorcycle-blueprints and plans.

That these tried-and-true motorcycle engines were used to power many of the micro-cars that came on the scene was the reason why the term "cycle cars" came to being. You will notice therefore, that most of the cars featured here run on just two bitty cylinders. Anemic, to be sure, compared with today's big capacity, high revving threes, fours, or even sixes from Yamaha, Suzuki, and Honda of Japan. Bike engines have come a long way today, to be sure! But all the same, these durable little twins were the reason for the successes enjoyed by a good number of the mini and micro-cars both on and off the race-circuit. So, many of them have over time become collectors' classics, commanding prices on a par with, or even higher that their more powerful siblings. I have gathered together here, for our show, as many of them as I can. I hope that they will help you see that there is definitely a niche market for these most practical types of automobiles right here in the US. Plus make you believe that good things can come in the smaller packages too!

From the first time I laid eyes on these little cars, I have been impressed by them. Why, I have always believed that it takes more engineering know-how to build small than large, not to mention light than heavy. With space at a premium, every component part will have to be custom designed to fit. If micro-electronics and tiny timepieces can work as wonderfully as they look, so can little cars. They can be veritable pocket-rockets.

Then, to a world that is scratching its head, and even tearing its hair out, like ours today,- worrying about what is going to happen when oil runs out, or is priced beyond our reach, the modern mini-or micro-car could very well be that pocket full of miracles we can dig deep into for solutions.

Think of it! The idea of these little cars being manufactured again. That is exciting! Then, the possibility of their coming into wide use, and thus helping us work our way out of our being so dependent on foreign oil is even more exciting. And perhaps the most exciting part would be the eventual rekindling of America's love affair with the automobile. Which of us would not love a car, which despite its smallness has the potential to prove itself a giant killer? One that is able to provide the masses with truly affordable transportation plus free the nation from the clutches of oil barons who could be in cahoots with people who are plotting 24/7 to do us in. Won't that revolutionize the automotive scene while at the same time, bring our whole nation together by putting everyone on the same page when it comes to giving OPEC its walking papers?

Read again the quote above regarding the Virgo Range micro-car. It "costs next to nothing, is effortlessly green, easy to park, and thread through city traffic, and is so simple that reliability is usually assured..." Now who would not be crazy about a car like that? Which red -hot and true-blue American, male or female would not get all taken up by a car this radical, though simple? An uncomplicated car that they can live with, open the hood and play with, and love, being that it is so cute! If you are not convinced, let me put it this way—who among us have not had cars which by their sheer weight and size alone have proved too much to handle? Have you had one leave you without help simply because it quit and wouldn't budge? The fact that cars here in the US are often referred to as "beasts" tells me that they can be quite a handful at times. Just go back to the time you got stuck and you could not move the @#$%! hulk one inch to save your life. It had obviously given you the "bug-off." The "expletives deleted!" This will not happen with a micro-car should it break. It could be pushed out of harm's way with little effort, to where you want it to sit until help arrives.

That the littler cars are so much more user-friendly alone would make them the first choice as grocery-getter, errand-runner, and resort or city scoot-about. It could well be the ideal retirement community automobile. A neat and not-too-tiny job built for American tastes would sell very well here. Just think of the many who live and work in the small towns and cities all over this country. They must number in the tens of millions. They would certainly not need anything large to get around in. A Virgo Range type car would serve very well. For those who live farther out in the suburbs, a slightly bigger two-seater that could be called on for quick duty would be perfect. Being something more substantial and speedier, it could even take the place of the countless gas-happy one-driver commuter vans and trucks we see on our roadways. As more and more people begin to appreciate how practical and easy on the pocketbook these smaller cars are, they will warm up to them. You bet the simple fact that these little cars are so eager to please would trigger an exponential upsurge in their popularity. Who wouldn't enjoy cars that do not have to be muscled around? Cars that are such fun to drive on the freeway, and so easy to park? Cars that do not ask much but for just a sip of gas to go places?

I will share with you a little later what sparked my interest in these little cars even though I grew up driving what my parents called "battleships"—the large cars Detroit put out. Indeed, I "happened" upon this wonderful "not-so-small" world of the mini and micro-cars quite by chance when I was on vacation in Holland a few years ago. The experience changed my thinking about cars.

From my earliest days, I have loved US cars. All the big, flashy dreamboats our Big Three made. I still do. Even after my "extra small car encounter of the best kind." Driving what many called "Detroit Iron" during my younger years gave me a rush, kind of. No one messed with anyone in a muscle car.

Like many here in America, I never had to go through all the hardships our European brethren experienced. So, from the time I got my own set of wheels, I shared with most people here, the "big is better" mindset. One of my favorite cars was the '66 Pontiac Bonneville two-door hardtop. This big beautiful doll was my baby. I shall forever hold it dear. Long and low, (and here, I must quote a good buddy of mine) with "rocket-ship lines," this car was the one I did 120 MPH in, one night when I won a drag race with a friend's Dodge Charger at a local strip! The ease with which it did that even surprised me. The gas pedal wasn't even floored with the speedo pegged. Its 389 cubic inch or 6.4-liter V-8 coupled to the AFB (aluminum four- barrel) carburetor gave it plenty of go power. So, it did not have to bellow or raise a ruckus to show off its muscles. It just quietly took charge. Without any fancy computer-assist too. Talk about impressive.

Still, the Bonneville was in every sense of the word, a "boat" for it was built more for comfort than anything else. Heavy and softly sprung, it was the perfect car for cruising. It would be hard for me to find a smoother and quieter operator than my Bonnie! Or a more spacey one. Its wide-track stance was accentuated by a superbly styled grille that gave it that low, lithesome look. Every line on this car flowed with designed-in harmony and balance not seen in any car then or now, I say.

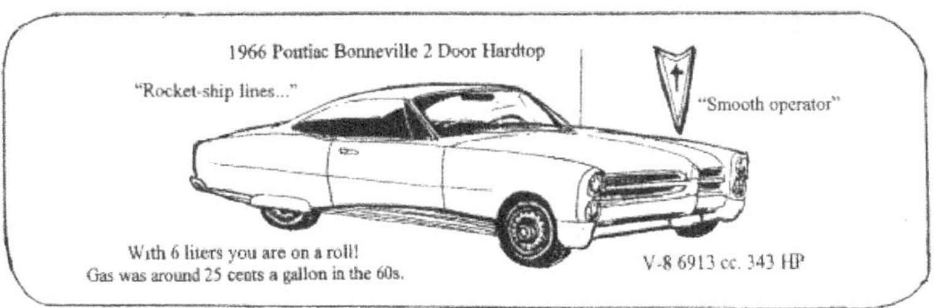

Check out its superb driving position. Love its bench-type front seat. Being a pillar-less hardtop, it gave one an almost unobstructed 360-degree view of the road coming and going. The sharply raked windshield and the huge, sweeping back-light gave one the feeling that one was riding with the top down all the time. What a car!

But really, what endeared it the most to me was that it could give me around 25 highway miles for every gallon of high-test when I went easy on the gas. Under 60 miles per hour, the secondary set of the four-barrel carburetor butterflies remained shut, and so, it basically ran as a car with twin carburetors. That was something special to me for I have always believed that efficiency counts most in any machine. For a high-end V-8 that weighed close to two tons to be able to get that kind of gas mileage was remarkable. But with gas costing around a quarter a gallon then, not many even so much as cared when I brought that point up to them.

I have always believed that Detroit should never have stopped making cars like it. American cars should always be large, long and low. Not down-sized or cost-reduced. With today's composite material, they can be built light and thus be as fuel-efficient as a smaller car. There is no need, whatsoever, for us to be fooling with tiny parking slots or narrow streets over here. We should rather, plan on resizing towns so that there is a generous proportion of everything in them. No two ways about it. There is plenty of open space here for expansion, and for us all to develop, from sea to shining sea. This is not Japan or Europe where there is little land left to do with. So, we should all be thinking BIG and building accordingly. Picture roadways so planned that they never need widening, spacious greens between communities, and room for everybody and their cars. That is my America!

Well, how times have changed! Today, we find our vision forcibly limited by factors beyond our control. We are once again, put on notice by the well-informed of the possibility of odd-even number-plate gas rationing. The prospect of having to wait in line for hours just to get to a gas pump like we did back during the "oil shock" of the seventies have to be troubling. There is no excuse for that! Are we not in a new millennium? Over 30 years have passed since the last time we had to queue up for a fill-up, and it seems that we have not learned from the experience. Are we such fools?

With all the damage Hurricanes Katrina and Rita have done to our Gulf shore refineries added to the gas pains the energy cartel is giving us, things are not looking good for the motoring public. Just think of how quickly we could all be plunged into a situation where once again, big cars and trucks, all certified gas hogs of little value when gas tops $6.00 a gallon, would simple be put out to pasture and left to rot, or be donated to charity and be shipped gratis, for use in some Christian mission outstations overseas.

But it doesn't have to happen if we take steps to change our mindset now. We could spare ourselves from getting caught by the next gas crunch—where we could very well be left with no choice, but to be put-puttering around in a moped, or worse, pedaling our bikes, just to get someplace. So, it would be a smart thing for us to start taking heed to what many of our European friends have been trying to tell us for a long time—that there is more to motoring than brute horsepower, that faster may not always be better, and bigger could be just that much more baggage to lug around. Bulk is basically more clunk and clutter. Nothing to brag about. Not in real life, for in real life, even top end means little, with speed limits all over the map. We all know from experience that size can equal waste. Isn't the bigger the trunk, the more the junk?

Thus, it is efficiency that should be considered above all else. Simply put, it is not how to get from A to B in the shortest time possible, never mind the gas, but how to use the least amount of it to do so. It is not packing as many horsepower into the largest engine we can shoehorn into the engine compartment but matching the required power output to the load that has to be carried. That takes doing.

As we enter into a time of increasing shortages in our world, be they contrived or not, we must, as responsible people, be willing to down-shift so as to make the best progress in our efforts at conserving our resources. We may be divided on the contention that our automobiles are the one big reason why we are in trouble, but we surely must agree that facts and figures do tell us that we Americans consume more gas than the rest of the world. Of every gallon we use, a good one-fifth could easily get wasted through needless idling, unplanned side-trips, shoddy maintenance of one's auto, piggish push-and-shove way of driving, or... You fill in the blank, for if I were to sit down and list all the little things I feel we should do to stop the hemorrhaging, I would need more than a couple of pages.

We are all aware that our country rolls on wheels, and that it has been on a roll. Everyone of us do indeed want to keep it rolling. But many of the wheels we ride to roll on are way off size. They take too much gas, and do not go the distance. Have not many of us indeed, taken issue with our carmakers about the gas-guzzlers they are foisting upon us? But they have not responded adequately, and so we must make it our business to find ways to address the problem. Just look at how increasingly more dependent we have become on foreign oil of late. See how OPEC is starting to swagger and talk tough about how they have every right to make us pay at the pump. Their take is: fork out the money if you want to drive! It doesn't take lots of smarts to know they will soon have us by the you-know-what! The recent up-tick in oil prices should signal red alert to all. It is time we wake up and smell the gas fumes!

What about our country's oil refineries, and our gas stations? We have been down on them a lot, and we are, mainly because of their cavalier attitudes concerning how their jacking up the prices at the pump will force us to cut back. Like it is in their interest to help us! But let us face it, the bottom line is still, supply and demand. Both have to be addressed. And the latter much more so, for has not the demand been forever: "More, more, more?" Sure, the oil barons are laughing all the way to the bank. They not only have us hooked, but they also have us all believing that, in essence, what we are paying for a gallon of gas is cheap! That we shouldn't be complaining even when the price is doubled. Yes, they know they can tell it to us for they are aware that our oil addiction is terminal. They are aware of our penchant for what Detroit has been pushing as "larger than life," too. So, they see no sense in slowing the profit taking even though a record-breaking 10 billion more of it has been stuffed into their coffers in the last quarter.

Let me venture to say this then. Even if Big Oil were given the go-ahead to open up the whole north country for oil exploration, you can be sure they would be turning over every rock, to see if there is a chance more millions could be pumped into their pockets. Until the last oil well is drained dry, the price of gas will continue to soar. Why, we will just be asking for more of it. Thus, all the talk about tapping our Arctic oil reserves to help matters means little. Why? Oil or no oil, the basic problem would remained unresolved, for we would not have learned to smarten up, and to conserve. We would remain as dumb and happy in our foolish fuel-wasting ways "easy-pickings" for the same greasy bunch of oilmen.

We all know that the promises of fuel-cell power, hybrid-drives and the high capacity batteries for a whole new generation of cars are just that—promises. GM, our largest, and indeed the world's largest auto-maker, as I type, may be working hard to bring us the miracle hydrogen fuel-cell car, but even if it is successful in doing so, (and I have my doubts as we know now how deep in money troubles it is.) it would be years before the thousands of fueling stations could be put on-line. Add to that the long years of waiting before all the supply logistics would get sorted out. No, it is not difficult for anyone to see that happier days will not be here anytime soon. That is not to say that I am giving the thumbs-down on GM. That despite all its problems. Not at all. Even though over 100 years have flown by since fuel-cells were invented, the very idea of zero-emission propulsion is exciting to me.

What about hybrid power, you ask? Is it not more practical? With so many hybrids coming to our showrooms soon, you would think that by the next decade, most of us will be zooming around in them. It seems that Uncle Sam himself is getting into the act, promoting their purchase by the masses with all kinds of tax incentives. The car dealers will not be far behind, we all know that, with their no interest, nothing down and nothing for the next six months, but you will pay forever plans for those who would drive them off their lots. To pump hybrid sales up to a fever pitch, many dealerships I am sure, would throw in a hefty price cut, for good measure, to make it appear like a deal that is too good to pass up. The push will be such that I would be willing to bet the greatly expanded lines of new hybrids from the larger car-makers across the seas will result in some introductory models being priced even lower than their gas-powered cousins. Then, the fact that hybrids are "green" too, beckons. For are we not all conservationists at heart? Their earth-friendliness would be stressed to no end. Yet, why are there many engineers still feverishly trying to perfect this method of propelling a car? It seems that the hybrid drive is still going through its developmental stages. And so it is.

The idea of hybrid power is not new. A Belgian carmaker by the name of Pieper was the first to build a practical gas-engine car with an electric motor assist in the early 1900s. Since that time, cars adopting this configuration in its various forms have come and gone. I saw with my own eyes a couple of very interesting ones at an electric car show in Philadelphia in the eighties. Both were one-of-a-kind home-builts. Though I was mightily impressed with the way they were put together, I came away with the feeling that they were still quite Rube Goldburg-ish. I can still see in my mind's eye the snake-pit of wires amidst the hundreds of different scrounged parts that were tied together within the close confines of their cluttered engine compartments. Each of the hybrids, like the electrics, must have been cobbled up from plans readily obtainable through Popular Mechanics or Mother Earth. One electric car, however, the YARE, stood out, and was in my opinion, head and shoulders above all the rest of the kit-car-like entrants. When it was unveiled, the "oohs" and the "ahhs" were something my dad would say: "not to be believed!" Though its performance was just about adequate, and its totally unconventional diamond-shaped chassis layout was rather strange, I thought it was worthy of note. So, I have included it here for you to see.

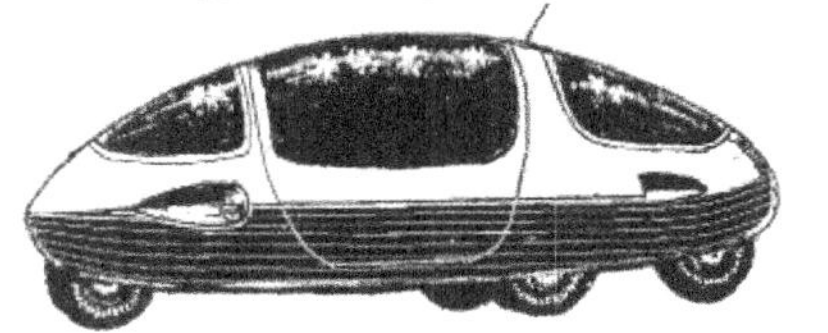

I shall never forget the YARE. Built by Dr. T.P. Kesling in 1978, this futuristic egg-shaped electric car was shown at the Philadelphia Electric Car Convention over 25 years ago. It could top 55 MPH and go 40 miles per charge.

Well, twenty years have flown since, and I am still hearing about more research and development being done on these two forms of automotive power—the hybrid and the pure electric. Being that the internal combustion gasoline engine is still king, the hybrid of course will take the front seat. Big oil will see to that. Argue all you want about how good and clean the electric car is, but that is the way it goes! Do you know that there is a report about how Mazda will be bringing out its own hybrid, the Premacy Hydrogen RE? Even though it can run on batteries alone, the stress is on its multi-fuel capabilities. And there is Subaru's high-tech R1e- another attempt at going all electric, with good figures we can check.

Toyota and Honda too, follow different paths in engine and drive management. The situation is not unlike when Beta and VHS were duking it out in the early years of video tape recording technology. I cannot help but wonder which hybrid drive will win out in the end. We'll soon see. Presently, Toyota seems to have a better and a more seamless way of blending gas and electric power. So, their Priuses are way out front in sales.

All the same, we have yet to get a satisfactory reply regarding what the high electromagnetic force-fields emanating from their hybrids can do to our health and wellness. That, I think, is what matters a great deal more at ground zero. If a tiny cell-phone antenna powered by a little matchbox size battery can cause problems between our ears, what about the heavy electromotive power put out by the electronics tied to hundreds of pounds of high-tech battery cells—just a few feet from our gonads? The field that the miles of coiled wires exerts has to be considerable!

If Uncle Sam is hoping that hybrid car ownership will take off stateside, in spite of its potential for problems, I would like to add this—just one routine re-battery job to get an older hybrid back on the road could cancel out every dollar of gas saved. Then, consider the cost of its gas-electric trans-axle. That alone will floor you. The Prius may be the market leader, but could it hold its position once past its prime, when its $3000 battery pack is depleted, and its $6500 trans-axle is shot? With all its high-tech this and that, the process of trouble-shooting it to replacing what is broken will be expensive, being that the job will have to be left to the experts,—to people trained in electronics as well as auto-mechanics. Why, dangerously high voltages are ever present in it. We have already been warned to stay clear of these hybrids when they get involved in an accident. Are you now beginning to see question marks written all over their hoods?

So, it could be many years before the hybrids will go mainstream. Which one of us will have the time to wait that long, let alone have the patience to take a bad one in for warranty work? Even a lifetime or 10 year/100,000-mile deal can be a bother if the car is basically a sickie. Simply put, until the general public can easily afford them, not to mention accept the risks that go with them, hybrids will not be making much of a difference. Like I said before, we have a well-educated car buying public here in the US. Once they get wind of the fact that our automakers are just looking to profit even more from the move, they will shy away. For this reason, I believe that despite all the hullabaloo about how many new makes of hybrids will be out in our car dealership soon, it will be a long time before they will be freeing us from our dependency on foreign oil.

I may seem to you to be a bearer of bad news, but I am not in anyway against hybrids. Indeed, I have always loved the idea of having a car with two propulsion systems. To never have to fear getting stuck on the road because the gas engine failed is just too wonderful to contemplate. To think that a simple turn of the switch the other way, and you are home free. Relish the feeling of be being forever liberated from having to wait for a tow-job. So, I would be rooting and tooting for all carmakers hooked on hybrids to keep working to bring out the best. And more, I would like to leave this thought for what it is worth—indeed, all gas-powered cars should have a new high-power pancake electric drive motor coupled between the engine and the transmission. Working synergistically with the engine, it could be turned on to move the car out of harm's way should it quit midstream in traffic or just to give it more pep. This simplest of hybrids could be the best—yet, as it leaves the matter of power-management in the hands of the driver. It will not cost much to implement, for no complicated automatic switching arrangement would be necessary. The small bank of batteries tucked out of the way in the truck would not take too much room either. Picture a gasoline powered car that is an electric at heart!

Until we have an effective way worked out, we need not put everything on hold, or go far to find the answer. We could go micro. So, let us time then travel to countries like Germany, France, England, and Japan to see how they got through their gas crises by going with their micro-cars. By opening our eyes to what sort of solution they have hit upon, we could be clued into finding practical ways to help ourselves cure our gas pains in a quick and easy manner.

It is for that reason that I have such a lot of pleasure checking out car magazines from all over the world. In my travels, I have often bought them as souvenirs. The car magazines from Asia and Europe are much like ours here, glossy and totally up-to-the-minute. They do reveal how absolutely car crazy all we earthlings are. We may want to believe that we in God-blessed America are the only ones into high-performance cars, but guess what, they have them too in Russia. Just as we have our Motown, they have their Nizhniy Novgorod. I counted no less that 125 different models the six major Russian car manufacturers make. Then, to those of us into concept cars, the Russians (and why not the Americans, I ask?) have a website that is all dedicated to that. Look up carstyling.ru.

So, it is plain to all that there are plenty of notes we can compare with our fellow car nuts from around the world. Surf the auto websites when you have the time. See for yourself that all that is talked about here is true. Like me, you could find yourself taken on a mind-blowing educational side-trip and be amazed!

One of my wild web rides took me to a page which showed the cars Mainland China makes. What an eye-opener! Who would have known that the 90 plus marques there produce over 250 models of cars every year? Though it may be true that some of their makes are merely "Chinese copies" (copies where even the mistakes get replicated) of cars made here in the US, as a recent TV news report claimed, many of their cars I saw do not appear to be mindless clones of anything I have seen stateside. Several, I thought are as jazzed up as those on our roads today. Perhaps too much for people who appreciate clean, uncluttered lines. That China will one day be the world's car maker is not difficult to contemplate.

Several mini and micros made there were recently brought to my attention by Mr. Erik van Ingen Schenau of China Motor Vehicle Documentation Center. (See page 130).

Nevertheless, I remain of the opinion that the drive by our Chinese carmakers to break into the world-wide market would take them on a very long and winding road. For one thing, their reasoning is quite different from ours. What is important to us—like durability, safety, and convenience, may not be regarded as much by them. At least it seems to me and many I know. And in their zeal to up production, they will often do so on the cheap, the standards be damned.

Their newest and first European import, a nicely proportioned and rugged-looking SUV called the Landwind has already gotten the thumbs-down in a crash test conducted in Holland. It is a shame. But, as all test results can be fudged, I will reserve judgment. With most of today's run-of-the-mill companies routinely stamping out cars that are solid, I cannot see why we should be expecting anything less of Mainland China's offerings. There is no place for a substandard product in this highly competitive market. No room for tin toys.

Still, let no one be fooled—for when one's number is up, the grim reaper will call. With God's okay, he will be right on time, with scythe in hand, and he will not be denied. He will be there, by the cozy comfort of one's bed, or right inside one's armored bunker, for he has prior claim. I can still remember the night these two area physicians, a rather well-known husband and wife team got their summons, right on the stretch of highway I drive on daily. They were returning early one morning from a vacation trip and heading home to Baltimore in their Hummer when they somehow busted across the median guard rail and got struck twice, head-on by tractor-trailers going north. They were both killed in the crash. Their kids survived, however, and were found wandering around the wreckage, dazed. So, it behooves us all to drive with care, and not on a dare. With life so full of the ironic, it would be folly to discount or defy the powers.

There is truly so much out there in the world of the automobile. Or of cars and drivers. Both the good and the bad. And more, the bad and the ugly. I have learned so many of life's lessons just watching the world go by, driving the thruways here in these United States. It has been sobering.

But let's just talk cars. All my years toying with tuning techniques and tinkering under the hood have given me many interesting insights into what this game is all about too, and how we ought to play it.

Therefore, I will never forget the day I received a pile of the Dutch AutoWeek in the mail from my relatives in Holland. What a windfall it was! Every few months now, I would get another installment of the oldies, dog-eared and paged through, with the crosswords all filled out. But all the same, goodies. With each copy so chuck full of useful info, this auto magazine must be the best of its kind in the world. Absolutely worthy of saving for reference.

Though not proficient in Dutch at all, I have been able to to pick up many good bits here and there. Just from the pictures alone, I have learned so much! No, it did not take me long to see how much better this humble tabloid-size weekly newsprint from Holland's little car capital is, compared with all the glossy, fancy auto magazines we get stateside. Here is at last, a publication that offers the motoring crowd the facts and figures that matters! It is not one that is merely a showcase for ads, ad nauseum. Or a forum for meaningless patter. You will not need to leaf through pages here, so jam-packed with, come-ons and money-grubbing offers that they are not numbered. And you will not be showered with an avalanche of renewal reply cards, or a clutter of coupons whenever you open it up. Ah, how often have we been abused in this way by what we car nuts pay good money for here.

The Dutch AutoWeek so far has been circumspect in this regard. Its business is about cars, cars, and more cars than you can name. You will find no army heavy battle tank being put through its paces here. Just cars, and cars that ordinary people drive. Many special interest cars get talked about too. Like the super classy and costly types, mind you. Even cars specially engineered down for the Third World. Cars that would seem a waste of time here in the U.S., being that they would not appeal to the twenty-something boy-racer crowd. But then, may I suggest that even the most unsophisticated make and model might yet be universally applauded one day as having contributed a goodly amount to the development of some far corners of the world by giving it wheel power? Imagine that,— simple, plain-jane cars designed to operate under the most primitive of conditions, winning their laurels, with millions and millions of happy owners cheering them on to take their places on the podium of the greats with cars like Germany's VW Beetle, France's Citroen 2CV, Britain's Mini-Minor, and even Japan's Toyotas and be forever remembered in auto-dom as having made a difference. You know I will be looking out for it.

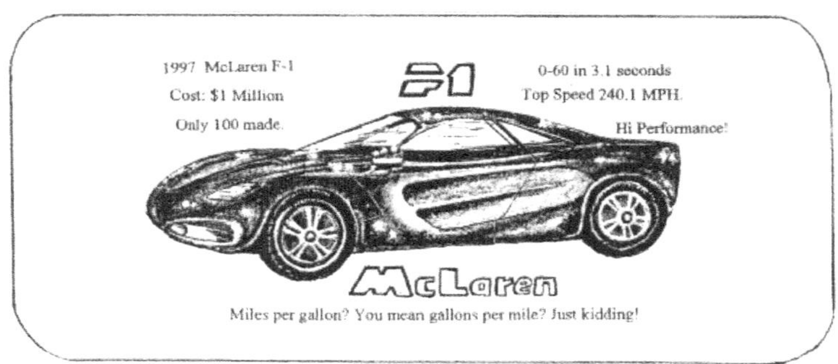

Allow me therefore, to ask: how many of the megabuck cars with their silly (and dangerous) show-off scissor doors and stupid do-nothing wings in back, not to mention a totally useless super top speed, that you saw in our car mags five years ago can you recall, let alone name? Well, let me refresh your memory regarding the 1997 McLaren F-1, a car that was lauded no end by the many blustering auto-journalists here. This so-called super-car was priced at a cool million, and was picked as the best of the 100 greatest cars made in the world by <Channel4.com>. Yet, it had to have a gold-lined engine bay to help keep it from overheating!

Sweet. Really, I have to say that this car has problems. Expensive problems. Problems no auto engineer worth his salt would want to be connected with. No wonder only 100 were made. Yet, it never fails, the simple bread-and-butter cars, the real people movers of society are often given just a quick once over and dismissed as unexciting and utterly ho-hum by our own automobile editors.

To be sure, there is a good number of these low-price, and low powered smaller cars out there—all featured in the Dutch AutoWeek that if imported here into the U.S., would sell very well. But they will not be given the time of day, being that they are too light to pass the crash tests mandated by government. Many importers deem them to be unprofitable to bring into the country for the cost of upgrading them and making them robust enough to stand up in a crash would be too high. Canada, however, do allow them in, but they have laws that will only let the ones that are over 15 years old in. Go figure that one out! Is that not like saying, "No, these little cars are too dangerous for our roads," when they really mean "too hazardous for our own auto sales industry?"

Does it not beg the question then: are we all going to be condemned to drive in morbid fear of those who are bent on turning their cars into assault weapons when they get behind the wheel? It looks like, does it not, that we are coming to a point where we have to be at the ready to dart and dodge in order to not get rammed at every intersection? Now, should everyone not act responsibly when they are behind the wheel? Must the motoring public have no choice but to drive with six airbags ready to deploy? Or be forever contemplating to trade in one's car for something more massive in order to be safe, cruising the highways? Will the day come when we will see "my car can beat up your car" bumper stickers everywhere? It is insane! Alas, it does appear that the ignition key has become some sort of a pass for many of the clue-less and mentally simple in our society to act like the devil, play at stunt driving, and burn enough rubber on a chase to turn our highways into a flaming one-way trip to hell.

How sad to have to be made to see that the day will soon come when the authorities, in order to rein in the irresponsible few will legislate to oblivion the automobile as we know it. The cars we will be driving in the future will be much like the slot cars we used to play with when we were kids—except that the slots they ride on will be electronic sensors and monitors embedded in the roadways, or radar governors that are programmed to throttle the Neanderthals at the controls or to warn them with alarm bells to quit it every time they try to push their way up somebody's tailpipe! We know already that the major trucking companies routinely track their fleet of tractor-trailers via the GPS system. What does that say of its employees? Would our cars be bar-coded and equipped with a spy-tech tracking-devices like it soon to keep us all in line? When that day comes, it would not be too far-fetch for us to regard our cars as mere appliances. Or worse, another of life's necessary evils. And driving one would no longer be fun then.

Well, I hope that it would never come to that. I enjoy driving too much to be looking forward to when I will have to let a robot-car take me everywhere! Driving is one of life's greatest pleasures. Imagine being able to get to where one wants to go without having to wait an eternity to check in for a boarding pass. Or to have to sit for hours in line on the tarmac, after one has been cleared for take-off? In this day and age, with car-makers everywhere putting out top performing products for all, I say that it should not be any problem for anyone with a set of car-keys to have all the fun in the world going places without having to put one's life on the line, or another's limb in danger.

Cars today are built to do their job well. Too well. With many of the latest models bristling with sensors, it's going to be scary, braving this new road-scape soon! It makes me wonder what these carmakers are thinking. We have enough distractions as it is with cars that have on-board computers that can keep us apprised when something goes amiss under the hood. With the advent of the GPS system, cars made by GM and equipped with "OnStar" can even talk to their respective service departments while, filling out their diagnostic files with what ails them before they signal their drivers and occupants! Commercials showing how they can track you down tell me that the day of the car thieves are numbered. For a long time now, we do not have to "tickle" the carburetor, much less choke it, as in days of yore, to get it going, like some of our British friends routinely do with their SU equipped cars.

To think that all this has come about in a little more than a hundred years—or since 1885, when the first car, a Mercedes Benz coughed and sputtered to life, and chug-chugged away in a cloud of smoke! It is more than amazing.

Even the tires on our cars are wonderful to contemplate. Consider the load they have to carry—under the most extreme of conditions. Think of the sizzles of summer and the frizzles of winter. And the abuses that get heaped upon abuse without mercy, especially when the mindless are behind the wheel. Yet, they keep rolling, without so much as a tire thumping pressure check every so often. I have seen so many cars and trucks on the road, lumbering along on under-inflated tires that I am to the point of checking my car's tires constantly and making sure they are at least a couple of pounds over—always. The many times I have had to drive around the bits and pieces of broken tread material during my commute tells me low tire pressure can kill more than tires. It may be argued that the tractor-trailers are largely to blame for all that litter. Being that it is human to abuse what does not belong to one, company-owned tractor-trailers are seldom well maintained by the wannabe-cowboys operating them. There is recently a bulletin circulating around showing the funny side of this bone of contention, hoping that it would help stop the neglect of these heavy haulers by their drivers. But seriously, the sharp rise in accidents caused by bigrigs ramming into cars do indicate that the problem is not going away anytime soon! If you are a fan of country singer Randy Travis, you will know that his latest hit, "Three Wooden Crosses" does resonate in my ears every time I see the many more monuments to shame and sorrow that have sprung up over the past year by the side of this highway I commute on.

I can recall quite a number of the crashes caused by 18-wheelers going wide, and blowing everything to kingdom come because their drivers either nodded off for a moment or because they were not paying attention and failed to hit the brakes early enough. Often, it was just that they were pushing overly hard. Excessive speed and following too close have been quoted so often by the highway patrol as the two main causes of the majority of these crashes. What else. When people drive for pay and perks, they will test the limits. A good number of truckers, I am sure, when pointed out, will simply spout

out expletives and be quick-in-your-face about how America's economy will grind to a halt if and when they quit. But hey, they are neither forced into jockeying trucks, nor do they drive for free. They signed on the dotted line and should be fully aware of the terrible conditions they have agreed to work under. How so? There are eye-in-the-sky satellites now maintaining a tight leash on drivers all 11 of the 14-hour contracted workday. Day after day. Simply put, no time for slackers, however sick or tired out, once clocked in. The run will be made. Period. Talk about what can happen on the highroads when push comes to shove. When nerves are jangled, look out! The disasters in the making, especially with more and more tuner-types and biker dudes out on our roads slicing and dicing with no regard to the 10 MPH per car buffer rule. There is an Internet column recommending four times that in the snow, mind you, and so, it is not too much for me to once again say how important it is for ALL to exercise caution while behind the wheel! Of course, first and foremost, to check one's tires, before going on the road.

It cannot be emphasized enough that the tires on our cars are more important than we know. Remember the tires Ford once specified for their Explorer SUVs years ago—to make them more appealing to the car-guys? They went about it this way, I am pretty darn sure of it. All "back-ass-ward," I say again. They should have been honest and gone with a bigger-than-big car program—from the ground up and tooled it up as their SUV. But no, being that the Explorer had been given the go-ahead by the management, they decided on the make-do route. So, to give their new truck a nice car ride, they got Firestone to design a softer tire for it. How stupid is that? Gas mileage too, was a concern, and so, they asked Firestone to just make the tire bigger around so it could roll farther for every gallon of gas. See how quickly you get a sense of what Ford was hoping to accomplish: make the softer tire do the work of the Explorer's truck-stiff springs. If it is not like making the tail wag the dog, what is? Any fool, even in those simpler times would be able to tell you that the mishmash would cause problems. For why, the softer tires would have to give more than the springs— every time it rolled around. Flexed to their limits, at high speeds, their treads would literally melt from the extreme heat generated, and separate. Picture this: a Ford Explorer driver on his high-chair, blasting down the highway, way over the posted speed (or the tires' rated speed) when the steering wheel suddenly gets wrenched from his wrist by thrashing tire treads. Tire rubber is a tough customer and will not give up without a fight. However shredded, it will flail its cat-o-nine-tails to the finish. Talk about unmitigated mayhem. Well, till today, Ford and Firestone have not fully recovered from all the negative publicity that resulted from the many fatal accidents caused by a case of mixing too little tire with too much truck. The moral? Take the time to build a good vehicle, or waste it in damage control!

So, I have never believed in jazzing up a car with those super low-profile tires with the run-flat look. Matched with some high-end Ben-Hur style alloy "chariot" wheels, they can cost $1800 a pop, so what's the deal? None, whatsoever. (Even with the crazy new spinning caps thrown in.) All cars have certain prescribed sizes of wheels and tires. Little leeway is given by the engineers who are paid big bucks to do the math for each car. Despite the fact that I myself have questioned the rationale of limiting a car to one particular size of tire, I say it is always better to be on the safe side here. Prove that for yourself by checking out the rims of any car that has been fitted with these skimpy after-market wheels and tires. See the dings that come from not having enough rubber to soften the blows? A few more rim-jobs and the ride is over. You bet factory specified tire rubber is a big part of the suspension system.

The Dutch AutoWeek illustrates this point in an interesting manner by showing the paw-prints of each tire they test—on paper. What a quick and effective way for its readership to see what goes when the rubber meets the road. I will include a few pictures culled from their test pages for you. I sure learned a lot about each tire just by studying its unique tread pattern. All the tires selected are put up against their competition six ways, in all weather, summer and winter, under all conditions. Their ability to hold the road is compared in a novel way, I thought, in a rough and rousting roundabout. From start-up to spin-out, what a wealth of data could be gotten without the car having to go far, or the magazine staff having to go around in circles.

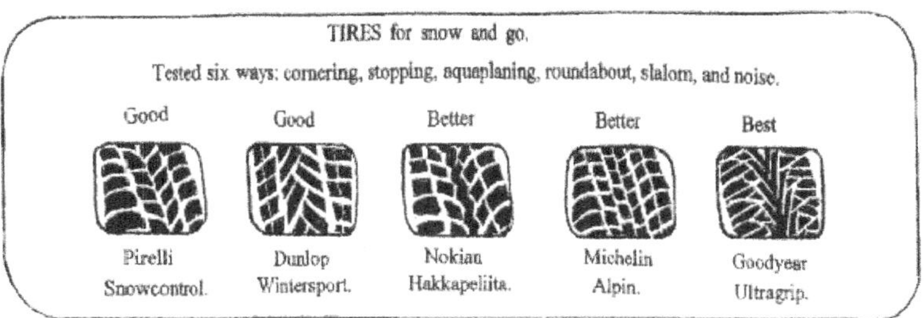

I have a friend who has an old classic collector's car that still rides on its original tires. Having heard so much about what dry-rot due to age can do to a tire in our local newspaper, I naturally had to take a good close look at the old rubbers on his car when he rolled up. Well, wonder or wonders, they looked perfect. That after fifty years! No sign of any damage due to dryrot. No cracks anywhere. Just the brand name we all know well: Michelin. They make the best radials.

Yet I have been told that our tire makers are talking about putting expiration dates on them. I wonder why. Could it be another ploy to pump up tire retail? Instigated by the many new and used tire shops, I bet, to jack up their profits. Or, could it be leading to something more sinister? A plot, perhaps, by the authorities to generate more revenue for highway maintenance? Surely it is not that our domestic products are somehow inferior.

Well, for the record, the first set of tires on my car—a 1998 Chevrolet Malibu, lasted over 110,000 miles. (The brakes too, as a matter of fact.) I was pleasantly surprised, for I have always been told that original equipment tires are usually the cheapest ones any carmaker will throw on their cars before they send them out the door. So, I can say with confidence that generally, today's tires can last more years than we know, and go the distance if we drive sensibly and follow the rules regarding their care and feeding. They will not on a whim, leave crisscrossing skid-marks clear across the dots and dashes of the hardball—from the merging to the passing lanes and back again unprovoked. If they fail to deliver, it is often because they have been pushed a bit too far by village idiots who are hell-bent on turning the daily commute into a demolition derby. The very people our highway patrol is on the lookout for, the "ignoranuses" who know little, and who care less—about cars, tires and really, about anyone else at all. If there is a group of people that needs to be reined in, this is it.

Apparently one local radio talk show personality is not on the same page with me here, for he got all huffy and puffy about how the police were getting more of these new traffic light cameras installed in our city. He was totally against them. And that even though the numbers of red-light runners have decreased by 40% (as reported in the latest issue of the Popular Mechanics,) in places where these cameras have been set up. He was not impressed even by the fact that the reason for the decline was that many more scofflaws have been put on notice. His talking points were that the camera suppliers were the people who made a killing off of the quotas of tickets the red-light cameras cranked out. He was ticked because he believed that the public should not have to be put through all the abuse just so enough traffic tickets got written. From all his rantings and ravings, I got a sense that he was the speed demon personified. Or, that he was after the ratings.

Be that as it may, the money thing, indeed, should have been honestly addressed from the start. Anything with a dollar sign will attract two-bit thieves and pickpockets, no doubt about it. Therefore, the problem is not with the cameras, but with the way the money that the cameras bring in is disbursed. Every penny collected should go straight to the state coffers, of course. Under armed couriers, what else. Is not assuring honesty still the best policy? From there, with proper accounting, the police department, the camera suppliers and all in the food chain would get their share. The feeding frenzy just has to be strictly controlled. Millions of dollars would be taken in every month from just the cameras covering the Interstate system itself, considering how speed-happy so many of our drivers are. Add to that the hundreds of thousands picked up from red-light runners in every busy city intersection, and you will see the ridiculously large company of people here who think they live in the land of the free for all. Observe for yourself, on any given day, how they will skirt the law when there are no police cruisers around, the hypocrites! So, I would not be surprised that the time will come, and soon, when there will be robot cameras looking on wherever there are cars. But it will happen, with countless millions of car-wielding psychopaths bucking for it. Already, the authorities have the means to single out speeders via the E-ZPass system. So, what's the big deal about cameras? None. Go check any high-tech surveillance equipment catalog, and you will see how tiny and unobstrusive these eye-in-your-face, day-and-night-watchers can be. You bet there will be "click-it and ticket" zones marked out for all accident-prone areas in your towns and cities, sooner than you know. They will do wonders to help stop the "carnage" on every intersection when their presence is publicly announced by cleverly positioned signs. The accidents they will prevent! The lives they will save! Then, they can in an instant, reach out like the long arm of the law to document and detail every asinine act of driver derring-do, and come, in these troublous times, to the aid of Homeland Security should one warrant an even closer look.

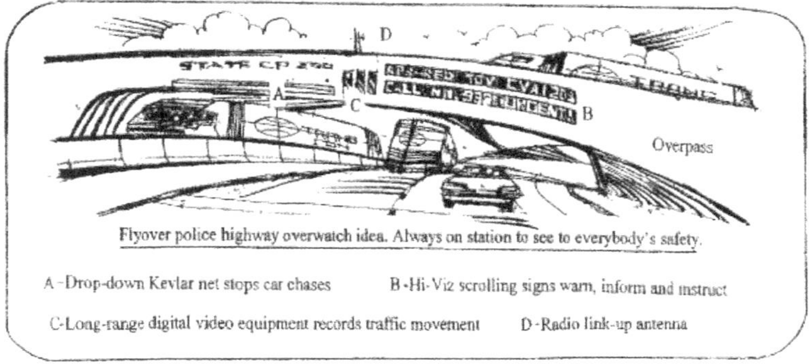

Flyover police highway overwatch idea. Always on station to see to everybody's safety.

A - Drop-down Kevlar net stops car chases

B - Hi-Viz scrolling signs warn, inform and instruct

C - Long-range digital video equipment records traffic movement

D - Radio link-up antenna

If this "Big Brother" stuff bothers you, I say, relax. We who are law abiding will have nothing to fear. There is a much higher hand that will separate the wheat from the chaff, without fail, in time. So, those who get tagged are the ones who consistently cross the line. As they have made it their habit to be defiant, they will eventually find driving on the wrong side of the road to be a rather dandy way to go. That, my friend, is when they will collide head-on with the law.

Come to think of it, the remark by a relative that the streets in America are paved with gold may yet be borne out because if this camera idea were to be implemented on the national level, I am willing to wager that in no time, we would be seeing the national debt get paid in full, thanks to our obliging scofflaw speeders. Even the funding the war on terror, and the rebuilding of New Orleans and the Gulf shores will get the stamp. And better still, the billions realized could go to provide everyone of us with free health care, while halving our house tax bills. Of course, you may think I am out of my frigging mind but do the math. Then, ask yourself how many here really, do indeed gripe about getting a robot-generated traffic ticket.

For sure, red light cameras will not only pay our way, and make our streets safer, but I know they will also open up a whole new era of law enforcement here in America! How? They will free up our police force for the job of going after the real crooks.

Talking about crooks, the ease with which they could break into a car and hot-wire it was interestingly dealt with in the Dutch AutoWeek more than a few times in the feature section. Stopwatches time each incursion with the accompanying photo shoot showing all the goings on as master car-thieves strut their stuff, ripping into the cars in the line-up. With gusto, like on candid camera. Then, the panel would point out what the respective automakers ought to look at, to make their cars more resistant to break-ins. Great stuff. But missing so far from our own car mags.

But one feature I thought was the best did not deal with cars freshly out of the factory, but with well-worn road-weary daily drivers, like my 260,000-mile-old Malibu. Talk about a real long-term test! That feature alone, I felt, must win the Dutch AutoWeek the most practical motorists' magazine award, hands down! (I made that trophy up, of course!) Within that few pages, one could get to compare notes with others regarding how one's ride should be in the area of performance after the odometer has turned over a few times. Car for car. With it on the lift, and its repair history opened up, both the good, and the not so good parts about the car would be pointed out. What a great way to address issues many auto service managers stateside like to dismiss as "inherent problems" so they could be let off the hook. Imagine Detroit having their design gremlins dragged out from under the hood for all to see! No way will they be able to get away with making a sub-standard product then, I say, once our car magazines here do a similar spread, week after week.

Another magazine department that I have yet to see in any competing publication is devoted to collision analysis and avoidance. This informative and instructive segment pulls out police files detailing recent car crashes and does an in-depth study of each. With photos and charts, the incident is re-enacted, so that the readership can learn what to do and what not to, while on the road.

Yes, I find that I have struck pay dirt by just mining the pages of my Dutch AutoWeek. It was what opened up the world of the mini and micro-cars to me, and it all came together when I went to Holland. Having first read about this tiny one-passenger car the Dutch is making for the handicapped in one issue, I was ever on the lookout for one the very moment I got there. Called "brommobile" in the Nederlands, which loosely translated is: "moped-mobile," it intrigued me no end, being that it is totally street-legal in spite of its small size. I wanted to know all about it. Wherever I went, I kept my eyes peeled for it.

My vigilance paid off one day when I was in the "centrum" of the city, with my sighting of this micro putt-putt pottering away leisurely among the many who were walking along the pavement in the closed-off part of the shopping district. The sole occupant, an old handicapped man had driven it up onto the promenade, and, guess what, no one even minded it! There were people walking around it, and it chugged along in step, moving smoothly with the crowd.

I went up to it for a closer look and saw how neat it was. Here was a car, scaled down to accommodate just one person, and yet, was by every definition of the word, a car. It had four wheels, a weather-tight cabin, and a windshield with wiper and all, just like any car we see on the road. I was impressed at how quiet it ran. Even as it sped up, the engine sounded like a sewing machine. Its exhaust emission was apparently very low, for neither I nor all those milling around it was bothered by fumes. As the little car forged ahead, the crowd simply made way to let it by. I have to take my hat off to the Dutch in how they regard all their fellows, right there. They have heart, as we say! Lots of heart. Here in the US, this would not happen. No tiny one-person car for the disabled would be allowed on the pavement, let alone on the highway. It would be run off the road, with impunity. In Holland, they can go everywhere. For there, even the bicycle is king. Amazing!

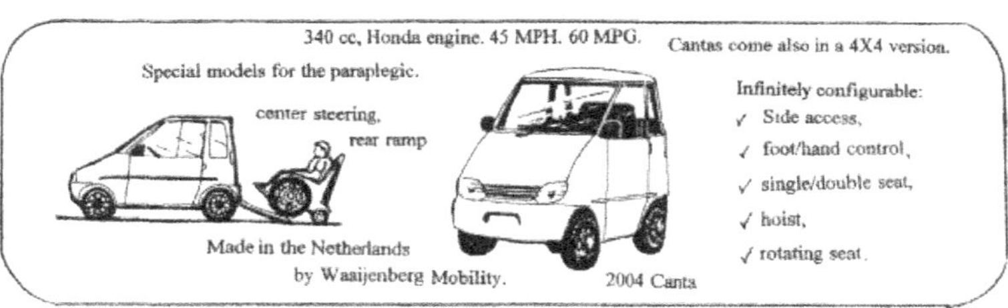

Now, if a car this size has a niche market in Holland, I can see why the slightly larger micros, like the Virgo Range is fast catching on. I talked about this little car earlier on, and have since, found out that the French and the Italians have been mass-producing a whole new generation of them for their own societies for already a good number of years. We all know they made those mini and micro-cars which were so popular in Europe during the fifties, but these are the new-style micro-cars, engineered to meet today's safety requirements, and to be totally reliable. They are speedy enough for commuting in, being gas or diesel powered, and yet, easy for 14-year-olds to operate as per their new regulations governing the use of these "quadricycles." Being that little four-wheeled cars are much safer to run, than scooters, they have become the way to get about for the younger population in Europe and the UK.

Here in America, these little cars may not be regarded as people movers in the same way, but their being so gas-efficient—with mileage figures in the 80 plus MPG range, they should be. Why, they could help us address the question of fuel consumption very well. Like immediately. They are absolutely practical for the millions who live and work in the cities and small towns across the country. With everyone who is unhappy with the high gas prices going micro, it will not take long at all before we would be slashing our foreign oil imports. There would be no waiting too, for any retro-fit to their fuel systems, should ethanol from corn become widely available in the future, although it is highly unlikely that our farmers will regard the venture to be worth the bother. Regardless, with many of these little cars powered by diesel engines, no major modifications would be necessary, should biodiesel become the fuel of choice one day. They are ready as of now, and perfect for the times. If our domestic car makers would tool up to make them, they would have so many good examples to go with.

Thus, we would not have to go hybrid, and be putting up with the high initial cost, or the new way of driving them if we switched to driving these mini or micro-cars today. There would be no need for us to wait for the hybrids to get debugged either. For all we know, it could take years before they would be as reliable and as cheap to buy as a regular gas-powered auto. And what is simpler or cheaper than a straightforward little gas-powered car? We would be silly to be thinking that Detroit is in any rush to roll out a hydrogen fuel-cell model the way things are going. They have their own agenda and it is not one that will be beneficial to us, believe you me. So, I would go with a micro-car any day if I could buy one. I know of a few who are sold on the idea, but because there are none available stateside, they have gone ahead to put their old gas-sipping Chevy Metros back on the road.

Honestly, I do not think we have many more years before our ever-increasing demand for foreign oil will blow its proverbial stack. With OPEC hinting about how they will cut back on oil production after 2008, we should begin to take steps to get ready for sky-high gasoline prices.

From the list of oil producing and exporting countries, we can gather that the majority of their oil ministers will be in no hurry to help us get through any kind of shortages. We know for a fact that some are even wishing us the worst! It would not be a stretch for me to say that there are many in that company of oily men right now, even as we speak, drooling, as they tally up the billions of dollars in potential profits, once a barrel of oil hits the $100 mark. So, the word to the wise is be aware, and prepare! Now is the time to go with the most fuel-efficient cars. And now is when we should be pushing for the micros to get built stateside. Before the rush for anything that saves gas heats up is when we should be shopping around for a something we can fall back on when the oil-stained rug gets pulled from under us.

OPEC - petroleum exporting countries:

Algeria
Indonesia
Iran
Iraq
Kuwait
Libya
Nigeria
Qatar
Saudi Arabia
United Arab Emirates
Venezuela

Own 2/3 of the world's proven oil reserves

<opecnews.com>

and Non -OPEC Countries:

Azerbaijan
Norway
Russia
UK
Canada
Mexico
USA
Oman
Yemen
Angola

Equatorial Guinea
Brazil
East Timor
Australia

Doing so would help the environment too, big time. All the micro-cars that are currently in production today are powered by small displacement engines that do not put out as much greenhouse gases as the huge belch-fires we see bellowing rudely around us today. Thus, a change-over to these littler cars would go a long way towards reducing air pollution. Their small size alone would mean that they would not add much to the problem of urban congestion. All positive and good!

With many of these cars able to cruise at 50 or 60 MPH, I know that they could conceivably be used by the average commuter in lieu of the family bus. In a 55 MPH zoned area, it should not have a problem keeping up with traffic. So, I would like to throw in my two cents' worth regarding the wisdom of keeping the highway speed limit set at an even 60 throughout the state. The mile-a-minute rule should rule. We will all fare the better for it. The 5 MPH leeway that goes with any speed limit will make it acceptable to the shameless habitually late "last-minute men" among us who must consistently push and shove to make it to work on time.

It is easy for all to see that at 60, there would be less of a chance for anyone to lose control at the wheel than at 80. The number of speeders will go way down from what I see everyday in my commute if this limit is rigorously enforced. Do, and over the long haul, there will be fewer ripped fenders and bumpers our highway maintenance people will have to pick off the asphalt, and body parts they will have to pull off the trees. Millions of dollars in police and EMS overtime will be saved as well. Not to mention the untold wasted hours our more careful motorists will as a result, be spared, creeping along in post-crash tie-ups.

Doing 60 instead of 65 will pay dividends too when it comes to gas savings. At anything over the 60 MPH mark, wind resistance becomes a big factor, and so, the added horsepower that has must be called upon to counter atmospheric drag. With it, goes plenty of gas, down the tubes. Picture a van or SUV bucking the wind and losing. Every time. Jellybeans are more efficient than bricks on the highways. The importance of a smooth, streamlined body for any vehicle going over 60 cannot be overemphasized.

One article I read about streamlining that have always stuck in my head showed how a tractor-trailer equipped with air-dams and full body skirting needed just 8 horses to keep it rolling at a constant speed. That really grabbed me! Another article about this dealt with grille shapes and sizes. A Jaguar XK-SS (See page 6) was put into a wind tunnel for aerodynamic testing and the scientists conducting the experiment concluded that all that Jag needed to scoop in every bit of cooling air its engine required was a grille-opening the size of a football. Wow! That is why we see so many Jaguars with their trademark oval grille.

Now, compare this finding with what our automakers are putting in front of many of the cars they are building. Take a look at the huge obscene truck-size grille on all the latest Dodge and Chryslers. Check out the new klutzy "300." I'll bet you its mileage figure would go up many points had its engineers toned down its anguished gape. Whatever happened to their new "Cab-Forward Look?"

I have always believed the idea in life is to be responsible for what we are given by the Almighty. That it is our duty to conserve our resources. And that it is important that we do our level best to not waste anything here on God's green earth. This book therefore is written to show that we can do quite a bit to advance this ideal with our cars. For do not so many of us consider our cars extensions of ourselves.

Here in the good old USA, cars are more than just to go from A to B in. Our cars have always been our dreamboats. We could custom order them in the sixties, straight from the factory with all the optional extras we desired—to our specifications. It used to be that we could trade our cars in every couple of years too, for a new one if we wanted to. Many of my older (and more well-heeled) friends did that! Then, a new Chevy Bel Air cost around $1500. Just a bit more than a Volkswagen Beetle, imagine that. A Caddy was in the $4,000 plus bracket. Sporty cars were the rage. Pickups were huge and station-wagons were so roomy 4X8 plywood panels could fit in back of them with no problem at all. Chevy Suburbans, the largest vans were what country and farm folks bought to haul everything, for SUVs and minivans were not even around.

Money was a lot bigger in value then, of course, but still... There were people making tons of it. Or not much at all. And there were those who were squandering their money as quickly as they made them too, or even before that, just like so many do today. The dollars we have now have by and large remained the same dollars that we had then. Almighty Greenbacks, all. Come to think of it, I am still spending roughly as much on what I need, except for gas. Most things today still do not cost a whole lot. Thankfully. So, I am inclined to say that with many people, a dollar is still a dollar. It can buy as much as you wanted, or as little. It is up to you. That is the beauty of life here in America. You have a choice—in everything. You can do something, about it too, or nothing at all. And you can be somebody too. Or nobody. It is all up to you.

In those simpler times, I did much of the maintenance on the several cars I had. (Yes, several. Used older cars were cheap. $500 could buy you a nice one then. Cream puffs were all in the $2,000 to $3,000 range! How times have changed.) Let me list: oil changes, lube jobs, tire rotations, hose, battery, starter and other small part replacements. I was quite a shade tree mechanic! Once upon a time, I even did a valve job on an Austin Mini. It turned out to be quite easy for the engine compartment was wide open. The head came off with no problem at all. The rest was all fun. Now, compare that with cars of today! If a valve job was that easy then, a tune up was even more so. A dwell-tachometer made it a cinch to get the spark gap and timing set just right. I was really into precision tuning, for I wanted my cars to run well, and to get every bit of go out of a tank of gas, even though gas was about a tenth of what it costs now.

Though times have changed, my thinking hasn't. I am just as into cars and everything that has to do with them even though I seldom muck around under the hood now. Cars today are better off not monkeyed with. With computer-controlled engine management, tune-ups involve nothing more than plug changes at 100,000-mile intervals, and so, they need little. Other than a routine 7,000-mile oil change with synthetic, and tire pressure check, they are largely maintenance free. Many are getting to the point where they are really quite self-regulating. On-board computers monitor their vital signs in real time, and schedule repairs, if needed. Despite all the recalls we hear of late, (shame on the companies that keep building bad cars) I am confident that one day a carmaker somewhere will succeed in rolling out a winner. One guaranteed to go 500,000 miles. So, I am perennially on the lookout for the best car made. Our Big Three had better get their act together and quit doing shoddy, substandard work if they want to remain competitive. They should be more responsive to the needs of the American motorists too, and start making the kinds of cars they want— in times like these.

Yes, I am very much into conserving my resources as ever. Over the years, I have tracked the rise and fall of merchandise prices and I have found that many of what should cost us an arm and a leg are way down, dirt cheap, while all the things that everyone of us here in this free country should not have to pay too much for are way up rip offs! We all know how expensive a DVD player was in 1999. It cost $800 then. Today, you could buy one for about $35. A five-mega-pixel digital camera that was listed at $700 in 2003.could be purchased for under $150 now. And a desktop computer, priced at close to $2000 in 1998 is regularly advertised at below $500 in the stores today. Some models can go for as little as $300. Color printers that can make copies better than the originals sell for lots less than $100. So, how is it that the relatively low-tech car has seen such a dramatic upswing in its MSRP in the last ten years? The onboard computer is no big deal, for they are dummies compared with the desktop one, and yet, car prices have gone through the roof. Even wannabe cars that are plainly junk have obscene stickers brazenly displayed. In the open too, for the dealerships know they have successfully gotten the status-struck over the "sticker shock" of years ago. Think about it!

I have a quick chart here to illustrate what I am saying. Hopefully, it will be the reality check we need to help us understand that something is going quite wrong here.

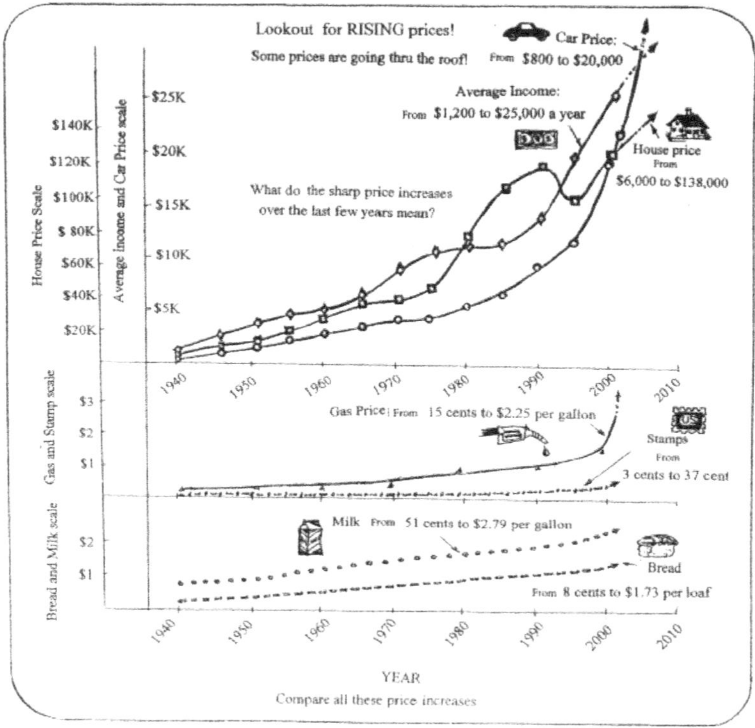

If the graph showing the leap in gasoline prices over the last few years has caught your eye, it has made my point. All my car talk about how we need a real gas-efficient vehicle to help free us from the clutches of the oil barons, and how the Big Three ought to be rethinking cars would not have gone by the wayside sounding like a plaintive voice crying in the waste howling wilderness. With more of us coming to see reason, it would be a matter of time before we would be able to get a strong message out to our car-makers that they have to justify the high prices they are asking for their cars. Imagine, $20,000 and more, for a car that is not really hugely different from one stamped out over 50 years ago! Shouldn't cars be easier to make now? The wheel must not have to be reinvented year after year, right? It has been over 100 years since the first car was made. You would think that Detroit should have got it down pat by now. I submit that cars are now much more complex, with their emissions and electronics add-ons. But with computers and robots doing most of the hard work there should be no mystery to it. Have we not been told of how automation will lower the cost of everything manufactured?

Yet it seems that the opposite is true. Thus, I cannot but put the finger on the robot manipulator as the cause of the cost increase.

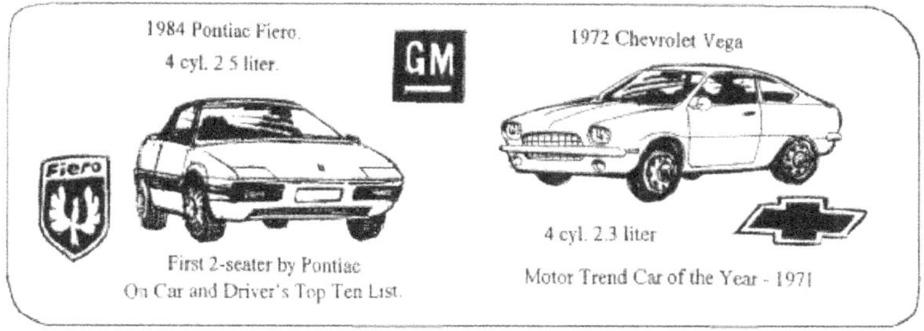

This aside about the Vega will show you what I mean. It was General Motor's first attempt at using robots to build a small car for the American public. It did well. Its little Chevy won the prestigious Motor Trend's "Car of the Year" award when it debuted in 1971. It was no small feat, for then, big cars ruled. The automotive presses raved about its great gas mileage and its many good points. A specially prepared factory car even went over 90 miles for every gallon of gas. But, alas, bad engine design resulted in constant overheating, which caused cylinder-head warpage and premature wear. The new technology "sprayed-on" cylinder wall idea did not pan out, and before long, this little-car-that-could got tagged as an "engineering lemon."

The same thing happened to the Fiero. This mini Pontiac sporty car had that super-car good looks about it. Its wedge-shape reminded me of 007's Lotus. I liked it so much that I bought one. (Although as one whose hobby is car styling, I felt its lines could have been refined some more, right on the drawing board so as to make it less of a FIAT X1/9 look-a-like.)

Anyway, as was the case with all first-year cars, it suffered from teething pains. Its problem was that its running gear was based on the rather lack-luster Chevy Citation. So, it had to go through numerous changes before it began to work right. I can still remember the many Fiero Club bulletins I had to consult to get my car to run. Or be "drivable." It was the first time I had a car with a silly-ass problem like that. A great company of those who were sold on the car's potential had banded together to help their fellow-Fiero-drivers sort through things as GM was very slow to address each problem that cropped up. It wasn't until 1986 when the best Fiero rolled off the production lines. But soon after, the whole line got shut down. Apparently, GM's bean-counters felt that sales were not good enough to justify keeping it. Does it not seem to you that profitability and not engineering excellence is driving this great car company? Any wonder why its market share has been slipping all these years? That it is on the verge of going belly-up? Had the Vega and Fiero been kept in production and constantly improved on, I am sure they would have attained true star status by now and become much sought after by all who want something that is not only economical and stylish, but also rock solid reliable. It's a pity that these two young upstarts were not given more time to develop into industry stalwarts. A definite loss to GM.

I have always believed that if you make a good car, they will come. Just look at the new Toyotas, or Hondas! Many are sold to happy customers without the need of a slick ad campaign many dealers use to help move their "excess inventory" off the lot to nudge them. GM, Ford, and Chrysler, (and the car magazine writers they pay off) may regard these Japanese "captive imports" as dull and unexciting, totally lacking in machismo, or sex, but just the same, Americans of all stripes and colors are snapping them up with a whoop and a holler. I have heard Big Three staffers belittle the Camry as having been designed by a committee, and therefore downright boring. But this car has broken every sales record there is for years, to become Toyota's top seller in the US! For why, it works. Despite its crooked tail pipe, may I add. You will see what I mean when you take a good look at it from behind. It may look funny, but the car buying public does not care, for it works, and who is to argue with them?

What about Honda? Their early Accords had problems. But each weak point was looked at by their engineers and corrected. So today, both Accords and Civics have become lauded by many to be the cars to buy for those looking for the best bang for their bucks. With so many Civic tuners booming around, it is not difficult for any of us to see how many of our younger drivers Honda is winning over. Years from now, I ask, will these "civic-minded" thirty-somethings be buying Corvettes or Vipers? The answer is clear.

CHAPTER TWO

Going Electric?

It is not at all surprising then, for Toyota and Honda to increase their market share in the US, year after year. I predict that they will be pushing for first and second place soon. Why? They know the kinds of cars we want, and they are not just willing, but eager to make them. Were they not the first out with the hybrids while Detroit was still kicking the idea around, hemming and hawing the whole way? By the time our Big Three are geared up to go, Japan's Big Two would have won the race.

The 2006s are here now. In Road and Track, I read that Toyota's new ninth-generation Corolla is just like last years.There is no need for it to be improved, the magazine tells me. (Though I humbly differ. But that is another matter.) Not surprising, considering this car has already been known as the best in its class. Dollar for dollar, no other car like it can equal it. I test drove one recently and found the car to be an absolute delight. The salesman was so sure about my buying it, that he simply handed me the keys and told me to take it out while he went on his lunch break. I checked the gas mileage figures posted in its spec sheet and was impressed. Being in the 38 MPG range, it handily beats out all the wannabe cars like the Hyundais, and the Kias. Its crisp and conservative three-box style has that timeless touch that will see it easily through another decade. Compare that with some of the ugly mutants out on the road, and you will know what I mean. Cars with that squashed, chopped and hunched look may be fashionable for awhile, but they will soon be seen as weird. Why, they are all basically pug-ugly. We will get tired of them in time. Just ask yourself if you will want to wear your hiking boots to the office everyday. Or if you feel comfortable doing your 9 to 5 in a cubicle someplace dressed as a race-car jock.

In the reliability department the Corolla excels too. All the big guys from Mercedes, BMW, Cadillac and Jaguar rank way below it in the charts. Like the Camry, the Corolla qualifies as a benchmark car. It is no wonder there are so many of them on the road.

So, to the friends of mine who advised me to go hybrid, I say, I have no need to. I can start saving money with the low-line Corolla right now. Its mileage is high enough. On a long trip, with less of the stop and go, its fuel mileage could even get close to that of a hybrid. And it would be on the road long after a hybrid is done.

However, if I were given the choice to go electric, I would. That is, if electric cars that can perform as well as gas powered cars were available, and at a price comparable to that of compact cars. A tall order. But then, with super space-age batteries and motors that can make any electric car go an unheard of 300 miles per charge manufactured every day now, is anything impossible?

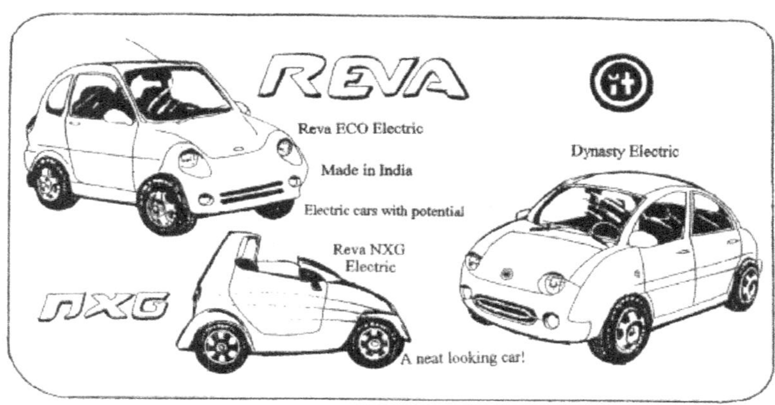

A range of 50 or 60 miles is usual with electric cars powered by automotive lead-acid batteries. There are, indeed, electrics in current production out in the showrooms according to the Internet. A bit of googling took me to this site which featured the little Revas. Developed in the U.S. and made in India, they use off-the-shelf deep-cycle golf-cart batteries. Both the NXG and the ECO look great. They are not at all dumpy looking, like the Citicars of the seventies. I am sure that if these two electrics were sold here in the

US, many of our city folks would buy them. The Dynasty Electric, also shown here, however, with a range of only 25 miles is best suited for use in college communities.

With the new super batteries using high-tech zinc-air, nickel-metal hydride and lithium-ion technologies, any electric car could have its range boosted considerably. But these batteries do not come cheap. Therefore, these electric cars, like the T-Zero, and the Fetish shown next have starting prices in the $30,000 range.

New motors too have been invented that can put out over 200 horsepower, and yet they weigh a mere 110 pounds. So, there could well be an electric car in my or your future! That is exciting, for I have always believed that going electric is the best way. We all know about the pluses. Zero pollution. Quiet, efficient power transmission that is almost magical in its smoothness. Take the T-Zero. Or the Venturi Fetish. They both can out-accelerate our hottest sports car— the Viper, which is, go from 0 to 60 MPH in 3.6 seconds. Electric motors put out maximum torque at start-up, is why! Without being hamstrung by all the frictional load imposed by the many piston rings, camshafts, and big end bearings, not to mention the timing chains and serpentine belts, an electric rotor can effortlessly spool up to top speed the moment it is switched on.

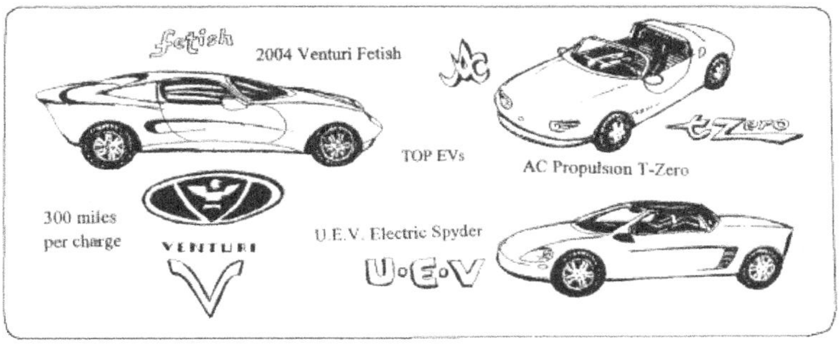

There is a Welsh engineering company that has developed a break-through, new-tech electric motor with no permanent magnets in it. Instead, timed pulses are used to spin its rotors with no losses of any kind up to 2500 revolutions. This means it could be coupled to power an electric car directly. Imagine the possibilities! No transmission means no shifting gears. Just step on it to go from zero to the max. The implications are awe-inspiring!

But alas, it would take an edict from the highest level to put this electric car concept in "D"—or "drive." I fear the reason why we are not seeing more electric cars being developed is because our carmakers are in bed with Big Oil. Perhaps you have read about how GM and Ford have both canceled their electric car projects. GM's EV-1 was built in 1997 and leased to over 800 happy people in sunny Southern California as an experiment. How happy you ask? Let me quote none other than Mr. Genius, Burt Rutan of SpaceShipOne himself. In an article about electric cars in the latest "Automobile" magazine he said: "...the EV-1 was the best car I ever owned." Well, I do echo his sentiments even though I have never owned an EV-1. My little toy battery powered R-C car is marvelous enough. I figure its scale speed to be easily over 200 MPH.

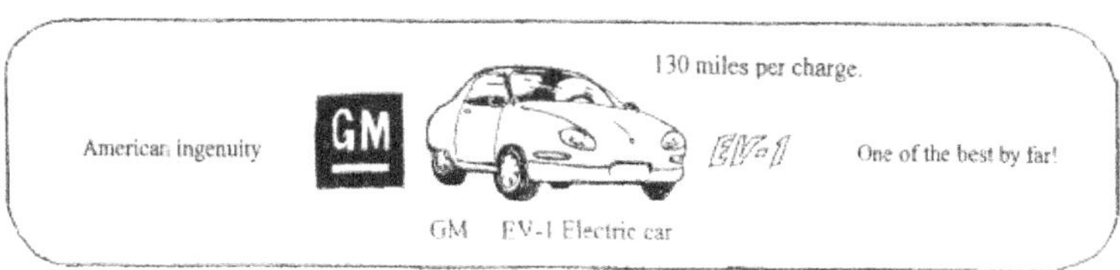

Indeed, the spacey EV-1 proved that it was feasible for drivers with short to medium commutes to go electric. The new nickel-metal hydride batteries in it gave it a range of 130 miles per charge! Twice the norm. Perfect for all. Yet, in 2003, when the lease ran out, the project was canned, and the cars crushed. Imagine that, a thoroughly good car, thrown away, with millions upon millions of R and D dollars. That is GM for you. (It is no wonder that more and more people are sure they bought up the 200 MPG carburetor blueprints some hot-shot engineer drew up years ago.) Ford's cute, micro-car-like TH!NK ran just as fine. Yet, it also had its rug pulled from under it. Go figure, and tell me if these two carmakers are not at all interested in going electric for the simple reason that there is much, much more money to be made in slapping together gas hogs?

You betcha! A successful electric car will result in such drastic cutbacks in gasoline use that OPEC itself will sit up and take note. Plus tear its hair. The need for oil changes alone will drop to such a point that our oil barons will be fainting from fear. Then, an electric car with a motor that works like a turbine can mean the demise of many segments of the automotive industry our automakers control. Why? There will be literally hundreds of thousands of cars cruising noiselessly around without the need for pistons, spark plugs, coils, distributors, cylinders, engine blocks, carburetors, exhaust pipes, mufflers, and all.... Consider the ramifications! Therefore, although I am 100% sold on going electric, I am not too hopeful that the day when we will be saying "Goodbye" to our gas stations will be happening soon. The oil lobby will make doubly sure of that. In league with Detroit, its avowed aim has always been to do whatever it takes to stay solidly entrenched in the business, and to promote the consumption of oil, and oil related products. Till the last barrel of crude gets refined, they will push their policies through, you mark my words. Therefore, the nod will be for yet larger gas-powered vehicles in the days to come, not for electric autos. Simply put, their game-plan is to keep making and selling as many of their gas guzzlers as possible, for as much as the marketplace will bear, what else. It's to "get while the getting is good," for they know that these super-sized "got-to-haves" of today will soon be the worthless "also-rans" of tomorrow.

In spite of all that, there will be cars like the YARE, quietly making their way out of garages here and there, freeing their owners and builders from the clutches of Big Oil, and giving them the (s)mileage only a select few who are resourceful and creative can appreciate. Electrics are indeed, the least costly way to drive, by far. Nothing can quite match it. Not even cars that run on biodiesel fuels. Or cars with hydrogen fuel-cells. An electric automobile that draws its power from batteries that can be recharged by the sun should be every electric car builder's aim. For the rest of us without the technical know-how or the wherewithal to go electric, we have to check elsewhere. Unfortunately.

So, we are back to our search again—for a car that will be a true gas-savior of the world!

As we move along, let us take a quick look at Ford's other good ideas. One, the Ghia Cockpit. This little three-wheeler ran off of a one-cylinder gas engine. Patterned after the Messerschmitt KR series micro-cars, it was made just for show in 1981. Now, tell me, were we not headed back on the right track then? As you can see, the Cockpit idea was not pulled out of thin air. All the same, if you are leery of trikes, Ford has the—Ka for you. Both the standard micro-size four-seater and the sporty StreetKa are made for Europe. An aunt of mine has one, and she loves it. I have seen the Ka myself, and let me say this, it is superbly engineered and packaged. So, I wonder about the wisdom of it not being produced and sold here. The StreetKa is a futuristic looking micro-sports car. The guy who designed it was truly inspired. What can I say but that I am sorry these two absolutely good little gas-sippers are lost to us?

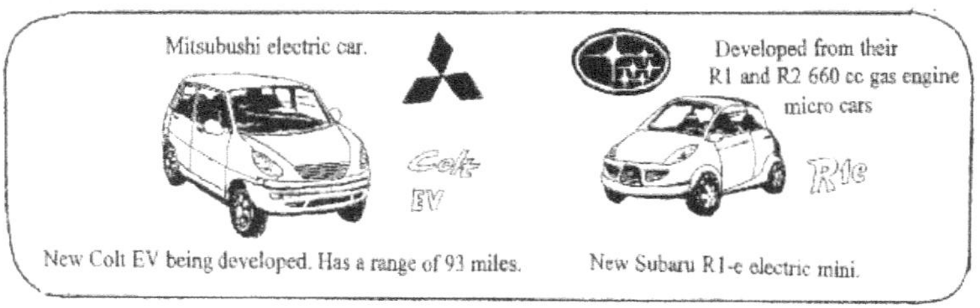

New Colt EV being developed. Has a range of 93 miles.   New Subaru R1-e electric mini.

I guess, it will be the Japanese then, who will once again step up to the plate. They are already waiting in the wings, with their electrics. (Did they not bring us the hybrid first? Thus, while we wait for Detroit to stop talking airily about the joys of hydrogen fueled cars, and start working on them, our Japanese friends will be busily getting their first production models ready for sale here. They know how our leaders are too mired in the political muck to be able to get Detroit to act.) They know too, how the bigwigs will balk at every suggestion they get off of their behinds. So, yes, the new Mitsubishi Colt EV electric car is even now, while we chat, being fine-tuned for its unveiling in 2010. Styled like a little minivan, it should be just the ticket for a small family looking for super economical transportation. With a range of 93 miles, it should be interesting to check out, and compare with Subaru's R1e, the other multi-mode gas and electric hybrid.

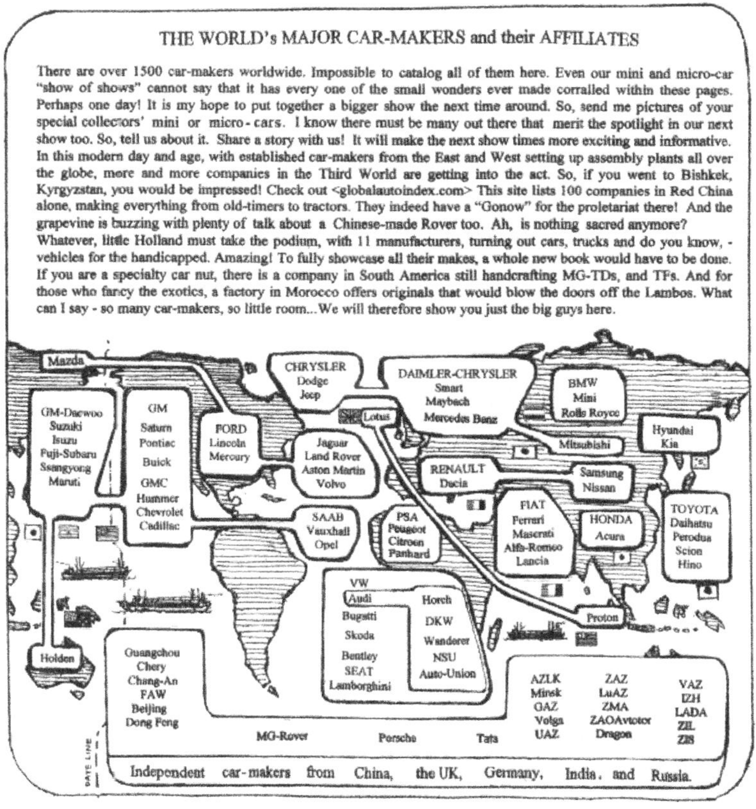

Derived from the successful gasoline powered R1 s micro-cars, Subaru's R1e hybrids, are going to get many to rethink cars. Its size alone will prove to all that good things still do come in small packages. Parked alongside a micro-car of the fifties, its ultra modern lines would be easy for one to appreciate. The immediate question would be: what makes it run? And more: what makes it so economical to run? How does it stack up, when it is lined up next to the micro-cars of the "Golden Era?"

To find out, let us step into the main section of our mini and micro-car show of shows.

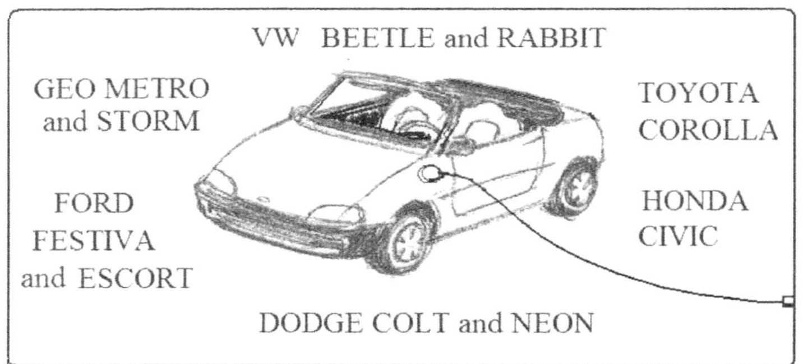

CHAPTER THREE

Going Small

Since my earliest days, I have admired the Germans for their technical know-how. That so many mini and micro-cars were designed and produced by them was therefore not a surprise to me. That desire for what is groundbreaking in the old Zwickau city of Martin Luther's Reformation must have been what fired up the engineers and innovators that gathered there in the early 1900s to establish Europe's motown. Count the many great German car marques that called Zwickau home: AWZ—Automobilwerke Zwickau, DKW—Dampf Kraft Wagen, Horch, and Sachsenring Trabant. All unfamiliar to you? No doubt, but surely not Volkswagen, and Audi, the two conglomerates all these old makes are grouped under today.

It was here that many of the mini and micro-cars of the fifties and sixties were manufactured. Innovation was the order of the day, and even the humble Trabant, maligned though it was, had something new to boast about. Its high-tech "duroplastic" body. Many dismissed this then state-of-the-art material as cheap pressed fiber. But I say its use demonstrated tremendous initiative, for steel was in short supply. Europe was just starting to recover from the war and so, most everything was rationed. The fact, therefore, that its engineers were not letting anything discourage them from forging ahead with new technologies must speak volumes about their talent and pluck. That after the terrible beating they took from our bombs.

Well, I know you may be wondering why I am kicking the showoff with this lemon, the Trabant. I do so because it is an interesting case in point. First, there has been worse cars. Forbes.com conducted a worst car survey and our Ford Pinto got 18 votes while the Trabant got 6. A list of poll results regarding the several cars featured in this book will follow.

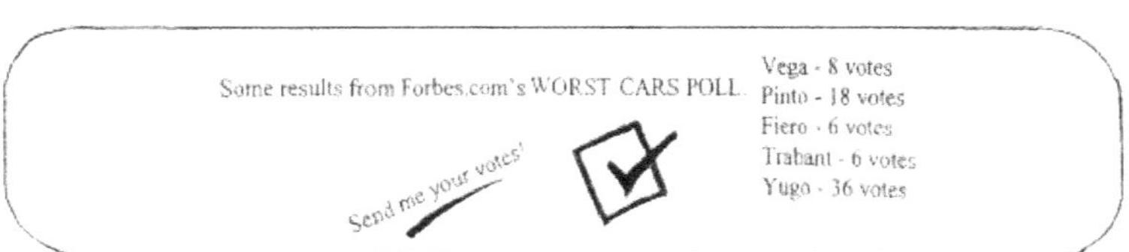

Second, though the Trabant may be considered by many here to be crude, it nevertheless outsold the much beloved British Morris Minor by more than two to one. Imagine that! And I have always regarded the Minor to be an all-time great. Its simple, straightforward design made it rugged enough for everybody and all types of driving situations in Europe. Although the first superhighways were built there, some of the cow-paths people drive on have to be seen to be believed.

Third, many in the Eastern Bloc swore by the Trabant. That, even when they had to wait over 10 years before they could save enough money to buy one. Still, over 3 million people did that. That was a huge number, and unlike us, they were not people who would take a car for granted. Then, how many of our own makes have sold that many? It is no wonder that the Trabant was dubbed the "National Car of the German Democratic Republic"—which basically is the same as, "The VW of East Germany." Let me quote an old codger: "The old Trabi—a simple, humble and beautiful toy!" Like millions of former Trabant owners, he was sad to see it go when VW took over its Zwickau works.

Before we move on from the Trabant, I would like to add that the first Trabant, the P-50 was intended to be a three-wheeler. Three-wheeled cars or rolleras were in the same class as motorcycles and were not as highly taxed. They cost so much less to own and operate as a result and became the common people's cars. Thus, many micro-cars of that time had three wheels. The 1958 Brutsch Mopetta was one, and it was about the smallest of cars, as you can see in this picture. Leave it to Egon Brutsch to come up with some of the wildest three and four-wheeled micros or kleinwagen as they were called in Germany. His V2Ns were shipped out here to buyers in the US, wouldn't you know.

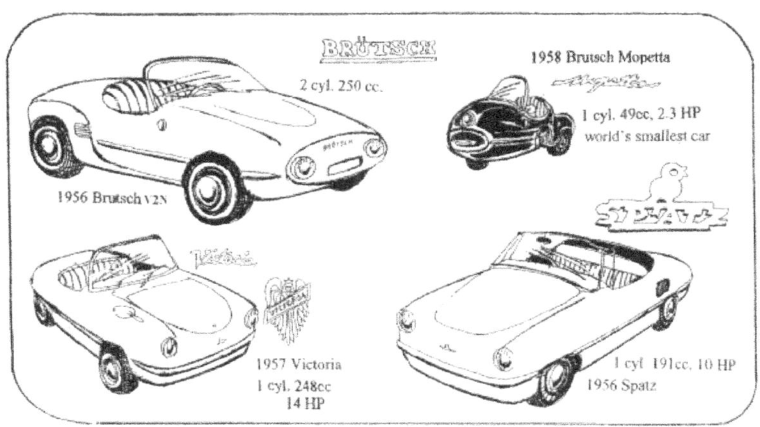

A couple of micro-car makers, namely Victoria Werke A.G., and BAG—Bayerische Autowerke GmbH, liked Brutsch's designs so much that they built cars around his platforms. Their smooth-looking variants like the Vic and Spatz were not bad at all.

The French too, the original car nuts, were not to be denied. The Societe Air Tourist, a licensee of America's Cessna airplane company came out with the Avolette, their copy of one of Brutsch's rolleras.

In contrast, Paul Kleinschnittger, a scrap aluminum dealer in Germany built his cars from the ground up, using sections of surplus cookpots for the front fenders. Although his tiny creations were just over 9 feet long, they were a hit, and many were sold throughout the world. It was said that they were exported to 22 countries. Made largely of aluminum, they were "as durable as they were inexpensive to buy." One, believe it or not, was recently featured in a Cadillac TV commercial to emphasize the Escalade's super size. It would not be difficult to picture the SUV riding around like the land yacht that it is with a little K-schnittger dingy hanging off its transom.

Another noteworthy company, one truly deserving of our applause simply because it went all the way with its less-is-more theme was France's Mochet. Its first cars—appropriately called "Velocars," came off the line as pedal-powered vehicles. What an extreme way to go to save gas! I feel the back-seat drivers' pain. Well, it did not take the company long to find a better way. Their improved Berline, a three-wheeler powered by a one-cylinder engine was snapped up by 3000 happy new motorists. The cheers and the collective sighs of relief must have gone out over the Eiffel Tower the day the Berline came out.

Many of these drivers moved up, in time to bigger and better four-wheeled micros. The Atlas "Babycar, made by Societe Industrielle de Livy" must have been intended for the richer folks. Its good looks won for it the fancy name of "Coccinelle," or "Ladybird" in French. Its curvy shape was perfect for a two-tone paint job. An interesting but old feature, however, was that it had a mower-type pull-start one-cylinder engine. From these humble beginnings came many of France's well-known cars.

Consider the French Panhard. One of the founding members of the automotive industry. Established in 1889 as Panhard et Levassor by René Panhard and Emile Levassor at about the time when the first Mercedes sputtered to life, it produced some of the most remarkable cars throughout its seventy-five plus years—until it was absorbed by Citroen in 1965. All the same, this illustrious French company wrote the book on series car production way before the other pioneering firms of its day. Its "Systeme Panhard" defined the automobile as a passenger carrying vehicle with four wheels in an age when many had three. It gave us also the Panhard rod, which is the track rod to us here in the US. Any sports car fan will know how important it is to always keep a car's four wheels aligned and firmly planted on the road. Every one of the cars this great automotive pioneering firm made—as featured in this Dutch classic car yearbook: De Onschatbare Klassieker (The Priceless Classics) were powered by flat-twins, or boxer engines of around 50 cubic inches. That was their trademark. And their trendsetting cars were unbeatable. These small capacity high-revving horizontally opposed engines were known for their dependable smooth running and good gas mileage. Their built-in vibration dampening design was what made them so good.

The Panhard Dyna 120, a small four-door family sedan was executed in the classic fifties style. Sporting the distinctive trade-mark Panhard grille it was already collectible the day it rolled out. Size-wise, it was smaller and lighter than a Beetle.

Then, we have the beautiful Panhard CD. Built in the sixties, and probably named after Charles Deutsch, of DB cars, its bullet-shaped body must have caught the attention of car nuts everywhere. Any car with that smooth an envelope must be really fuel-efficient. The CD proved that out, and more. It showed that it could really haul—with just a two-cylinder 848cc unit of 50 HP. It could easily go 100 MPH. Now, does that not tell us that brute horsepower is not all there is? Rather, good auto-engineering. We have a car here, that truly merits a closer look by any company, or anybody interested in the production of an ultra high fuel mileage car for this day and age. It takes real skill to design and build cars that perform without having to rely on as many cylinders as you have fingers and toes to count. It is no mystery to any at all, that hundreds and hundreds of horsepower will get you the speed and acceleration you want. We all know too, that such an engine will also run one to the nuthouse with its need of care. Or drive one to the poorhouse with its constant need of feeding.

The bigger Panhard Dyna 54s and 59s, made in the fifties also had the same air-cooled flat twins of 848cc capacity for power. Yet they could go over 80 MPH and give 40 plus MPG. Their ultra smooth, aerodynamic shape boasting a drag coefficient of .26, coupled with their light, aluminum bodies were the reasons why. How light, you ask. Much lighter than a Beetle, although they were longer by well over a foot, being full-size four-door family sedans. We will therefore not include them in our show. But I will have pictures of them and other beautiful cars that I consider to be greats for your enjoyment in another car book soon.

Panhard's little Dyna Junior has always been one of my favorites. Look at how well-balanced its design. This little car measured 12 feet long, and yet had the look of a much larger car. With a two-cylinder 745cc engine, it could top 90 MPH, and deliver over 40 MPG. If a fifties car could do all this, does it not stand to reason that we in this millennium, with all our technological know-how should be able to make something that can perform twice as great? Picture a car with the CD's shape and the Junior's style.

Indeed, the more powerful DB cars made by Deutsch and Bonnet often participated in European Formula racing. But their mini-cars equipped with little engines were what left many race fans awestruck. Imagine, with just a 954cc twin putting out 72 HP, the DB Super Ralley built in 1960 was able to top 115 MPH!

If speed is what you are after, consider the DB Coach—a car Charles Deutsch and René Bonnet built in partnership with Panhard. It's smooth, lines show how aware they were of the crucial part streamlining plays in a low-powered car. Just stick your hand out the car window when you are doing sixty and you will see. By facing your palm squarely against the wind you will quickly appreciate the force with which a car has to grapple with as it pushes ahead. Yet, with just a two-cylinder engine of 851cc, the Coach could do close to 100 MPH, and so, many of these jelly bean smooth cars were raced. Let me quote a reviewer: "Despite their diminutive size, these mostly blue cars are amazingly fast."

Panhard's durability was the reason why the 1956 Arista Passy also, was based on its running gear. This stylish personal car, about the size of the VW Beetle was made from 1956 to 1963. Being much lighter, it could do 135 KPH or 84 MPH on its little air-cooled 2-cylinder 848cc.motor. Its handling must have been good, for like all the Panhards featured here, it had front-wheel drive.

For those who preferred convertibles, Rovin, a small independent French carmaker offered the tiny D4. It had the classic look of a toy car. To be more specific, a tin toy car. Coupes were also available, but the open cars were neater. The top-down look somehow made the little two-seater better looking. One commentator said that it was "well built and delightfully styled." I whole-heartedly agree. A recent old car magazine had a close-up photo of an older Rovin with bullet-style headlamps. Even with them sticking out, the car looked fine. No complicated, compound curves or sculpting, marred its smooth fender. The simple grille consisted of three chrome strips. How hard is it to make one like it today? A basic micro-car that runs well, gives 50-plus miles to every gallon gas and is easy to service could be produced using parts readily available off the shelf. It does not have to be loaded with all the unnecessary and costly bells and whistles. A slightly larger fiberglass body with the straight, clean lines of the D4 would be no problem to lay-up. Voila, a sell-out!

Several micro-cars which were much unlike the ones considered mainstream are worth a look at. The French Inter 175A, a three-wheeled, tandem two-seater was steered by a handlebar. Built in 1955 by SNCAN—Societe Nationale de Construction Aero Nautique, it was France's answer to the highly successful (though rather weird-looking) German-made Messerschmitt KR micro-cars. Thus, the basic similarities. Its strange cyclops headlight arrangement, however, made it look kind of weird. The public must not have liked that, because the Inters never sold as well as the Messerschmitts. Or the Isettas. Collectors, all the same, love it, however, for its unique style.

Heinkel, Germany's other premier warplane builder, famous for their bombers, was in due time, permitted to reopen its manufacturing facilities for the civilian market after the Second World War, and so, the Kabine. It combined the best features of both the Messerschmitt and the Isetta. Being more spacious and stable, it sold well. But its production was curtailed in 1958 when Heinkel was given the go-ahead to resume work on aircraft development. The rights to the little bubble car were sold to Trojan which continued making the Kabine under the "Trike" name from 1958 to 1963.

The VELAM, like the BMW 300, was also an Iso Isetta, but license-built in France. With sales of the Isetta, going crazy everywhere in Europe, it was only natural for car-makers able to set up the production lines and pay the licensing fees to want to corner some of the action. Iso or Isothermal, the Italian company behind the Isetta was not at all unhappy about that as it would make its car available widely to a world that was hungry for the lowest cost way to get about. Therefore, the "Vehicule Leger A Moteur," or VELAM, which is French for "light vehicle with motor."

The Iso Isettas were also built under license by companies in England, Belgium Spain and Brazil. A total of over 30,000 of these "Urkel cars" were made from 1954 to 1964. Remember the TV series, "Family Matters?" Renzo Rivolta, the one-time refrigerator manufacturer, and chief of Iso never would have dreamed that his funny looking little "rolling egg" as the Isetta had come to be fondly referred to by many of its fanciers, could make him so famous! That despite the many who must have commented on how utterly "cool," the way he had put his surplus refrigerator doors to use!

And how! Fast forward to page 108 and you will see that mighty BMW of Germany too got into stamping out their version of the Isetta, the 300. Flashing the well-known blue and white roundel, this crazy little car was everywhere, even at the race and rally circuits in Europe.

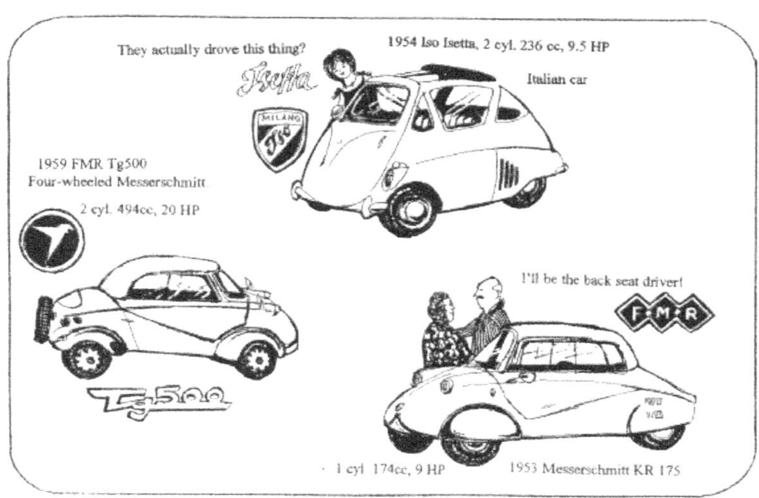

The top spot in the world of microcars, however, must go to Messerschmitt. Its TG500 (The "TG" stood for "Tourenfahrzeug Gelandesport" which meant "touring vehicle, cross-country sport") was the most highly priced of all micro-cars ever made. Built by FMR (Fahrzeug und Maschinenbau Regensburg) in 1959, it had the best features of all the three-wheeled kabinenrollers Professor

Messerschmitt made, and more. It rode on four wheels, and that made it much more car-like, even though it retained its unique enclosed motorcycle feel. You would know what I am talking about if you took a ride in one, for this little fighter-plane-wannabe could fly "low" at 80 MPH. Over 45,000 of them were made from 1953 to 1964. That is over ten years! Hundreds of them have been restored today and many can be seen in car shows here and in Europe.

One engineer, Carl Jurish must have taken too many "flights" in both the Heinkel and the Messerschmitt. I am not implying that he DUI'd—meaning that he "drove under the influence" here, but that he must have been so thrilled by the "roller-coaster rides" he took in them that he decided to build his own kabinenroller. He too wanted something better, and so, from parts he took out of a motorcycle sidecar, and some micros, he put together his Motoplan. This little rocket was shipped way out here from Europe for sale in New York City back in the late fifties. The novel way you had to open it up to get in alone made this micro like something out of Flash Gordon!

Another roller of note that came from Germany during the early fifties was the Fuldamobil. It was powered by the same engine that had made the Messerschmitt KR201 so popular. Designed and built by Elektromaschinenbau Fulda, GmbH, it became an instant success. Shaped like a regular car, this three-wheeler could carry a small family of four. So, it met the needs of many families that clamored for a cheap and practical way to get about. It came with an optional sunroof and was rather well-appointed for an economy car. The demand for it was so great that it was built continuously for twenty years, from 1950 to

1970, the longest production run of any micro-car. Many thousands were manufactured under license in India (where it was called the Bambi), Chile, Greece, and England.

The British version of the Fuldamobil, the Nobel, was the most notable in that its chassis was made by the same company that built the Titanic. And would you believe, its fiberglass body was molded by the famous Bristol Aircraft Company. No doubt, little cars were big business, to the heavyweights.

A thought: should they not be that to our Big Three today also? It would be no trouble for them to set up a line just to turn out a "back-to-basics" kind of car—for people who are not into anything fancy. With today's high technology in engines and structures, it would not take much for a thoroughly safe and roadworthy sub-subcompact car to be designed and stamped out. It could be based on any of the little cars that have done well during the past.

1955 Kroboth All-wetterroller   1 cyl. 174cc, 9 HP

Gustav Kroboth, another German engineer, must have got a bright idea when he found a VW windshield. It was just the part he needed to get his "All-wetteroller" up and rolling. He wanted to build a tiny two-seat car that would do an even better job of saving gas than the Beetle. At about 9 feet long, and powered by a 9 HP gas engine, his little convertible was an all-weather roller that could.

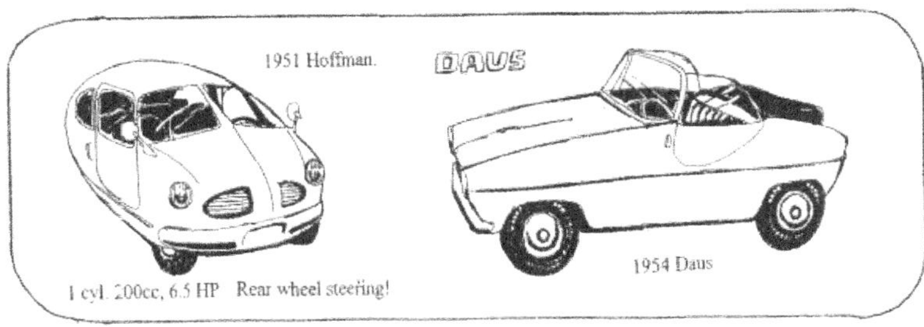

Otto Daus too, shared the same daydreams and took time off from his mundane job with Vidal and Sohn, a small company that made three-wheeled commercial vehicles to build his little sports car. His idea, though simple and straightforward, had the makings of a winner. The Sparrow, an electric made here, may be technologically superior, but it just did not have the "drop head" gorgeous kind of excitement that the Daus had.

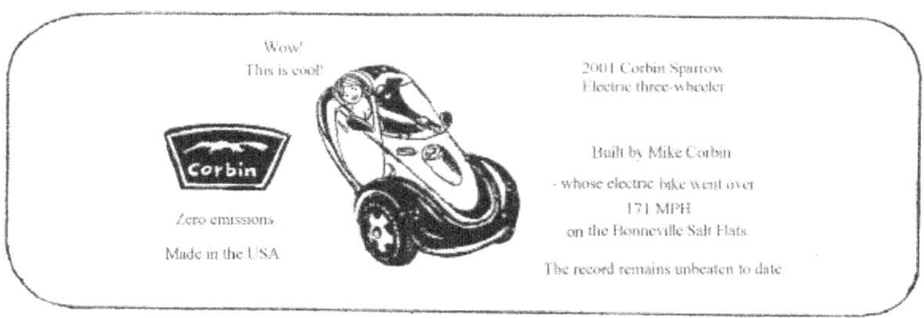

The 1951 Hoffman might strike you as being much more futuristic than both the Daus and the Sparrow, being shaped like a Buckminster-Fuller "spaceship," but its development did not go beyond the first stage. Its rear-wheel steering must have been what doomed it from the start.

For sure, German engineers in the fifties were an innovative bunch. And they knew how to make much of the little they had on hand during those difficult post-war days. The 1946 Champion 400 showed that well. Manufactured in 1946, one year after the end of the war, it embodied many interesting new ideas. Its front and rear panels were made from identical pressings. Even the doors could be installed with few modifications, left or right. What economy of design! This car would conceivably require a total of three main pressings to build. The semi-circular side window glass alone was noteworthy. It rolled along a curved track using an ultra-light rack and pinion arrangement. But alas, with the economy of many countries in shambles, the 400 did not sell as well as anticipated. Being priced rather high, it could not compete with the simpler and more ordinary cars, and so, in due time, the Champion car company was taken over by Maico, a competing micro-car maker. Maico's pretty 1957 500 Sports is shown here.

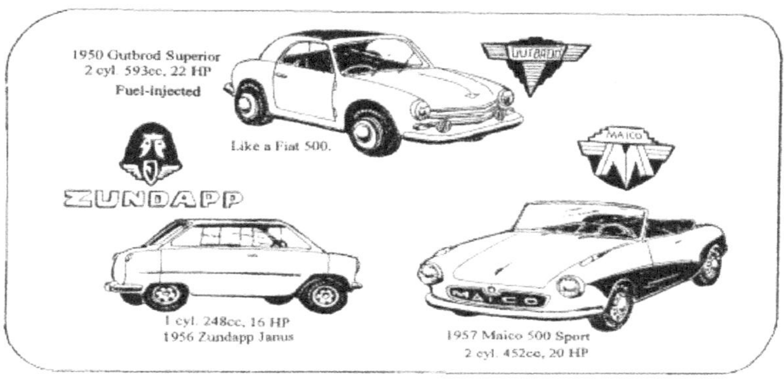

Like the Champion 400, the Gutbrod was a standout. Being fuel injected by Bosch alone made it special. Picture a 50-year-old car with today's modern fuel management hardware. Its creators, brothers Walter and Wilhelm were truly way ahead of everybody else, even though they sought just to make "an everyday car for the masses—but one that was superior to all other small cars." Therefore, the "Superior." An example of this car is still proudly displayed today at the world-famous Bosch showroom in Germany.

Another interesting German concept was the use of back-to-back seating in an auto to save space. We have heard the saying, "Less is more," and the Zundapp company believed they could work with that. So, the Janus. It proved out the theory well, for it could fit four people into a car which was just 9.5 feet long. Built in 1956, the Janus was the Isetta taken a couple of steps farther, being that it had both a front and rear-facing door for exit and entry. Well, I have to say that Zundapp was trying too hard when its aim was to market a car that was better than the Isettas, and the Fuldamobils. Had they put people first when they did the design renderings, they would have been infinitely more successful. Who among us would not want to sit up front, facing in the direction we are going? The Janus was fine mechanically. All the four little 250cc cars that were entered in the tough 2000-plus mile Liege-Brescia-Liege rally in 1958 did well. They proved their worth indeed, when they finished in fine form and won the team prize.

I hear that there is a start-up small car company in Germany that is presently developing something based on this space-saving concept. Check out the Loremo website: www.loremo.com. I am inclined to think that the car's two-headed Janus-style "dos-a-dos" seating arrangement will not fly. From the drawings alone, as presented by its sales department, I could see the idea suffering the same "opposites subtract" fate. Picture if you will, a crisis of major proportions should one be involved in a bumper-to-bumper head or tail-ender while creeping along, even at a snail's pace in a rush-hour traffic jam! Then, God forbid, should a fire flare up in the engine located between the seats could either occupant get out in time? I am afraid not. Enough said.

Now an aside, to see what our Spanish engineers have cobbled up.

Spain also built a number of micro-cars in the fifties. All were interesting examples of what the motoring public of that time wanted. Economy of operation, price, safety, durability, and of course, style, and good looks.

Take the FGL Alicante. It was named after its engineer, Francisco Gomez Lopez of Alicante. This neat little two-seat micro sports car was well received when it came out in 1959.   The Biscuter (sometimes called Biscooter) Pegasin was a miniature version of the beautiful and speedy Spanish Ferrari—the Pegaso.

Spain's longer-lived production micro-cars were of course, the SIATAs. This company, Societa Italiana Applicazioni Transformazioni Automobilistiche, made cars based on the Italian FIATs. As they were highly successful in the field of auto racing, tuning accessories were their forte. All the cars they came out with could be categorized as high performance. And stylish, like the Spyder 500 which was bodied by Bertone. You would never know that it was an economy car powered by a two-cylinder motor of under 500cc just by looking at it.

The 1954 SIATA Mitzi was much plainer, as it was a classic econobox. Powered by a two-cylinder engine of under 400cc, this car would be perfect for those looking for the least expensive way to get around. Its basic three-box layout was both practical and easy to refine. If further developed, it could have been a great little runabout! Built stronger and a mite larger, and powered with a 500cc engine, it would make a fine commuter car.

I am of the opinion that the PTV had to be the star micro-car of Spain, although it was not the best seller. 5000 of them were made, and they all came with snazzy two-tone paint scheme. In case you are wondering, the three initials came from Perramon,Tacho, and Vila, the three caballeros of Automoviles Utilitarios S.A. What was amazing to me was the fact that this great-looking car was powered by a little one-cylinder, 13 HP gas engine.

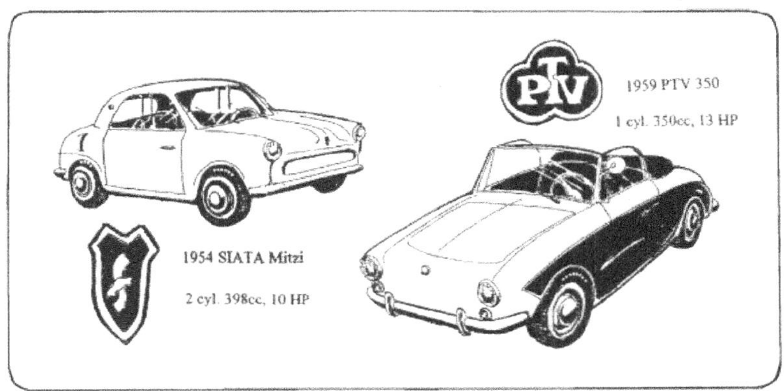

Perhaps the smallest fully enclosed car ever, was the Peel P50. This mass-produced micro-car used the tried-and-true DKW 49cc motor. DKW was then the largest maker of motorcycles in the world, and its engines often were specified to provide the motive power for many of the little cars that were made in the fifties and sixties. Some of the engines had been manufactured down through the decades relatively unchanged. So tried and true they were.

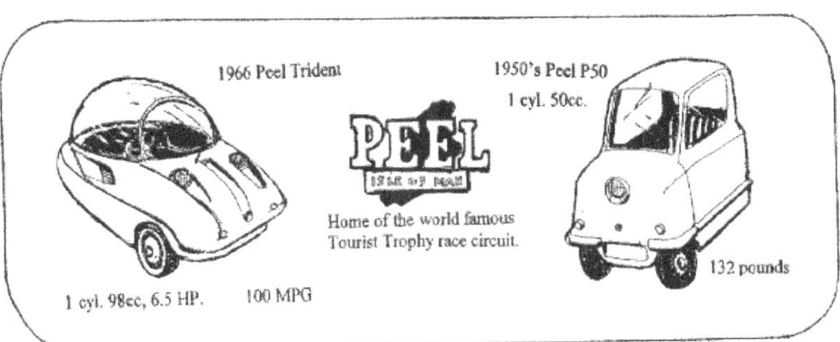

Ah, if only that could be said for our present-day engines! One big reason why the Peel P50 chair-in-a-box car was able to garner the kind of following was because it was so thrifty. Many swore that it made driving "cheaper than walking." The larger Trident was every bit like a bubble car for it came with a clear plastic top. Its engine was twice the size of the P50, at 98cc, and that made it quite nimble. Its rounded streamlined shape must have been the reason why some Trident owners raced them. All the same, this was one heck of a micro-car, for it cost so little to operate.

In one micro-car club magazine, I read about the Trident being replicated. That is great good news to all those of us who are perennial fanciers of these little super economical cars. I am sure there are many who would put up good money to buy one!

Today, with the move by some of our car-makers to go retro, I am persuaded that it would not be a bad idea for them to reproduce cars that were once-upon-a-time mileage champs. Cars like the Ford Falcon or Chevy II would be great to bring back. To be sure, together with the heavy 300, Chrysler should have reintroduced the Valiant as its new lightweight champ and won for itself much acclaim. A thought.

Another British three-wheeled micro which was not unlike the Peels was the Scootacar. Huntslet Engineering, a locomotive manufacturer produced it from 1957 to 1964. The Scootacar used the same seating and steering arrangement as the Messerschmitt. However, it stood taller and had a regular-size car door which made getting in and out of it much easier. With a length of only about 7 feet, it was ideal in the city. Its 9 HP engine gave it a range of 80 miles per gallon of gas. When we take into consideration that it cost just about US$520 in England then, and only US$10 for it to be registered, we can see right away how inexpensive it was—to buy and run.

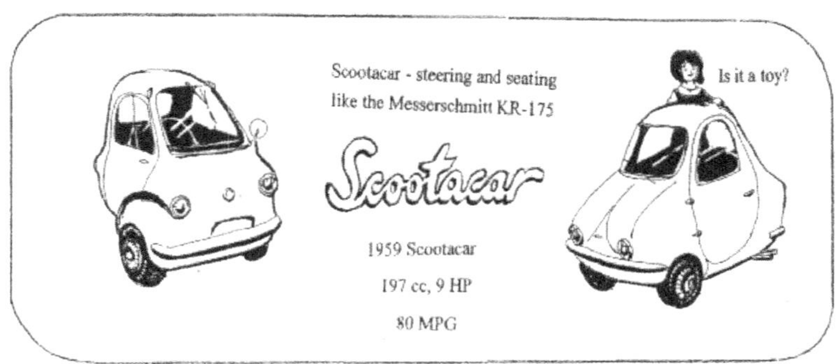

Three-wheelers have thus been popular for generations with a big sector of the motoring public in England. Not only are the thrifty sold on them, there are but also a great many dyed-in-the-wool zealots who believe that four wheels equal one too many! Bond and

Reliant will always have that corner of the market then. Even AC, famous for its sports cars, has a share in it with its Petite.

However, as the Reliants were rather large, and were powered by bigger four-cylinder engines, we will not include them in our mini and micro-car show. But I have to make mention of the fact that the Reliant Company was at one time the second-largest manufacturers of cars, small, medium, and large, in the UK. And by "large," I mean cars like the regular size four-wheeled ones we drive. Their Regals sold to the tune of 20,000 each year. The smaller three-wheeled Robins which went out of production for a short while because the company decided to "move up" and import the fancier micros from France, are once again being rolled out. Brought back by popular demand they are here to stay. With a top speed of 90 MPH and an excellent gas mileage figure of close to 90 MPG, it has to be the first choice for many motorists who do not see the need to put up with the high cost of registering a four-wheeled car with the Ministry of Transportation just to get from one place to another.

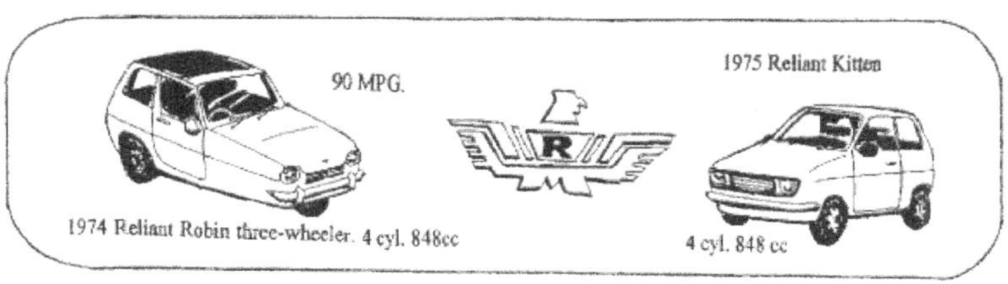

The Reliant company also made a four-wheeled version of the Robin in 1975. Called the Kitten, it was a plain but excellent little car for those who prefer to drive something more conventional.

The three-wheeled Bonds, from the Minicar to the Bug have always looked kind of awkward to me. (Had company bean counters been paging through some of Laurie Bond's renderings? Sometimes, the automotive sales and accounting staff can do so much to stifle the design department! In their quest to sell a product at maximum profit, they will do a D&C on all that they deem unnecessary regarding anything that is on the drawing board. You will know what I mean when we get to the section on the Berkeleys.) The utilitarian Bond Minicars were to my eyes, not styled to please at all. They were plain and basic cars which appealed to the no-nonsense crowd. The early models were quite bare-bones, with soap-box derby wire-bobbin steering system, antique rope-pull starter and an engine-drive-wheel set-up that looked like it came straight from a powered wheelbarrow. But few complained, for it could turn on a dime, and it took only pennies to operate. Minicar owners loved it for it could go 90 miles for each gallon of gas.

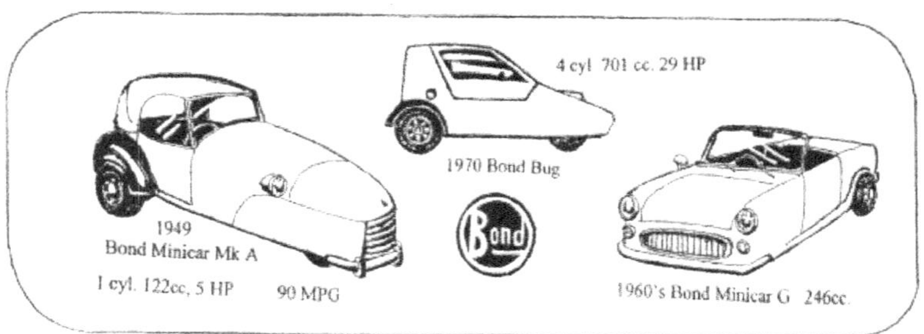

Many of us must be quite familiar with the AC car company's Ace. Known as the Shelby Cobra stateside, this superbly designed sports car had been so successful in racing that it has been copied by many kit-car manufacturers. I was rather intrigued therefore, by the fact that the humble, three-wheeled Petite was also built by AC. It must have been odd for a company whose name is synonymous with horsepower and speed to be making their own line of econocar. How it calls to mind what BMW had to do when it was fighting to stay solvent in the fifties. Could it be that the Petite was AC's Isetta?

I cannot help but wonder what if AC had bought up the Berkeley Car Company when word got around that its owner, Charles Panter was in financial straits. I am sure many good things would have come out of that. The Berkeley Sport's strong family resemblance to the AC Ace alone would have made it a natural for the company to hunker down and concentrate on making the new super-hot race-winning little car they had acquired better than ever. Imagine how well AC would be doing in all areas of mini and micro-car production and sales, with the popular little Berkeley T-60 three-wheeler complementing their Petite lines and their own works Berkeley 492s becoming the ones to beat on the 500 and 750cc race circuits! With their Ace taking the lead and setting the pace, I am certain all the race circuits at home and abroad would be such fun to watch.

Ever since I first laid eyes on the Berkeley sports cars, I have liked them. Designed by Lawrence Bond of Bond Minicar fame, the Berkeley Sports with its modern sports car lines was a smash hit the day it was shown to the public at the London Earl's Court in 1956. Priced at under 500 English pounds, (about US$1100) and billed as the lowest priced sports car in the world, it was the talk of the town.

Built by Charles Panter, owner of Berkeley Coachwork, the largest caravan maker in Europe, this fiberglass bodied sports car was, according to an Autosport reporter, "an entirely new kind of car." It "bristled with novel features." An Australian car magazine that tested out the Berkeley down under even called it a "miniature masterpiece." The sporting magazine, "Wheels" was not all bluster when it reported that the Berkeley embodied the latest technical know-how in glass-reinforced-plastic stressed-skin auto body construction. With its body and frame built as a unit, it was remarkably strong and light. Then, its transverse engine orientation was most innovative, predating the Austin 7 or Morris Mini by three years. So simple was the car's layout that Histomobile, the magazine said: "its ingenious approach to simplification rivals that of the 2CV" which we all know is the paragon of design simplicity. But truly, without the need of fuel, oil or water pumps, the Berkeley must take the top prize.

Weighing in at about 800 pounds, it could go over 60 MPH and return 60 MPG with its two-cylinder, 328cc air-cooled, two-stroke Excelsior motorcycle engine. A larger three-cylinder, 492cc powered model, capable of getting the little car up to 100 MPH was also made. It was raced with much success. At the Monza 12-hour race, it came in first in the 500cc Gran Turismo class. An article in the April 17, 1959 issue of Autocar exclaimed: "An outstanding and unexpected British victory was scored by the Berkeley, the more convincing because it was achieved in a straight fight with the best Italian exponents, and at record speed." Over 902 miles were covered at an average speed of 75.6 MPH. That was quite a feat considering the fact that the Berkeleys in the race had to stop twice as often for gas. Their fuel tanks could just hold over 3 gallons. Later, in the September of the same year, as was reported in an article titled "Short and Sharp" written by Nigel Halliday, it won the Monza Grand Prix, which was the "Grand Premio D'Italia," with panache, beating the racing FIATs by four laps.

At Verona, as at the 12-hour race at Monza, and in the 1958 Mille Miglia, Berkeleys came through with flying colors too, and according to the report in the Fifties Superbomb Sporting Cars' February '83 issue, "shocked the establishment by beating the works

FIATs and Stanguellinis." In 1959, it won the J Production class, its class, in the 12-hour enduro at the Mille Miglia, where, in an article titled: "The Berkeley—a little giant killer," by John Woods: "it outran, out-cornered, and out-handled everything from MGs to Jaguars." Closer to home, at Silverstone, it too was "victorious against many larger and more powerful cars." Be they in hill-climbs, in England or Ireland, this smallest of race cars "completely filled the 750cc and 500cc racing classes," and as was reported in the September 1956 copy of Autosport, "went incredibly fast."

Berkeleys were sold in many parts of the world and it raced stateside also, with good success, winning the SCCA (Sports Car Club of America) Modified Cars I class in 1958, 1960 and 1961 according to the Brooklands Road Test's: "Berkeley Sportscars." Go to the coldplugs.com website.

With race wins like these, it was logical for its builders to specify larger engines for this little "Fifties Super-bomb," and so in 1959, Berkeleys were upgraded with four-stroke Royal Enfield engines. With the even more potent 692cc Constellation, top speed was upped to around 105 MPH for the B-105 model. The increased power, however, lowered gas mileage slightly, to the 45 MPG range. The changes also made it necessary for the hood, and the grille of the car to be redesigned to accommodate the taller power unit.

What made this little car so popular, I think, was its eye-pleasing great looks. Its pretty face coupled with its sporty ways made it a winner. Its design adapted very well to a three-wheeled platform, and so the T-60 version. In time, a stretched four-seat variant called the Foursome was produced in rather limited numbers. The three-wheeled version, however, was what sold the most, with over

2500 made. It had all the creature comforts and safety of a regular car with none of the high registration fees associated with one. Small and cozy, with side-by-side seating, it appealed greatly to motorcyclists looking to move up from their happy-go-lucky two-wheeling days into something more suited for couples. Here was a car that made a lot of sense to them, being low in cost to operate, and good to go in any weather. With lots of room for things to boot.

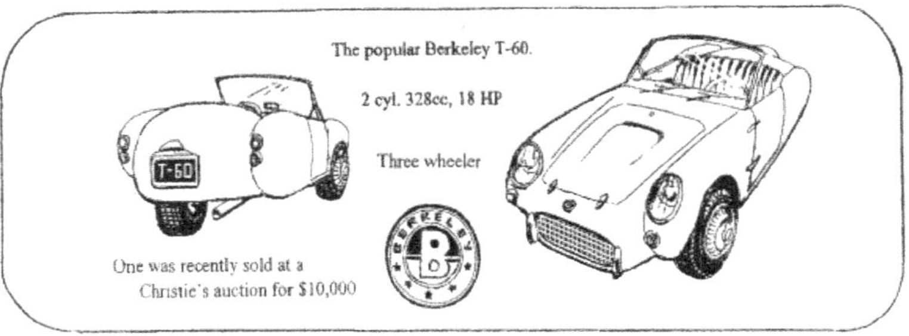

The interest in this tiny gas-saver, seems to be as strong as ever today. There is an article in the May 2006 issue of Classic Motor Monthly extolling the Berkeley's amazing race wins, mind you! It is no wonder that although almost 50 years have flown by since the last Berkeley was produced, there are still many who fancy driving a car like it. With gas prices soaring and automobiles becoming less user-friendly, it would be a refreshing change if a carmaker somewhere were to retro the Berkeley—to celebrate its Jubilee!

There is a company in England that is able to supply a completely layered-up fiberglass body for it for about $3500. So, are there any takers?

With today's high technology, it would not be difficult at all to put a car such as the Berkeley Sports back in production. This most basic design has the potential of being an all-time great, if scaled up a little, and tweaked to give dependable service. In this day and age, many drivers prefer a car that is as easy to get in and out of as it is reliable. We do indeed live in the gas and go generation! The low-slung sportsters of yesterday are often regarded as more of a bother. Today, few drivers enjoy being pinned down in a semi-reclined position seated, unable to look out of the car with ease. Good all-round visibility from the driver's seat is once again, a definite plus.

To be sure, there would be plenty of high-tech replacement components that could be used to make the new car work better and run stronger. The body alone could be made of the new composite materials now widely used in aircraft construction to good results. The weight savings alone would mean that even with a small two-cylinder engine providing the power, its performance figures would be more than adequate.

Another British micro-car that captured my imagination was the Frisky. Like its contemporary, the Berkeley, it was a product of the times. England was caught in a gas crunch during the mid-fifties, and overnight, the market for smaller and more fuel-efficient cars opened up. Raymond Flower, a racecar driver was the one who broached the idea of producing the Frisky to Lawrence Robson, chairman of Henry Meadows Ltd., engine maker to famous car companies like Lagonda and Frazer-Nash. In his letter to me, Henry J. Meadows the grandson of the senior Henry Meadows, said that Gordon Bedson, the Export Sales Manager was then tasked with its design.

The first Frisky proved too complex for production, and so, a restyled model, powered by a 325cc Villiers two-stroke was introduced at the 1957 London Motor Show. It was able to top 60 MPH and it gave 60 MPG. Both three and four-wheeled models were produced. But unfortunately, sales never took off. That, despite Michelotti, the famous Italian car-stylist giving the Frisky the "millionaire look." Production came to a halt in 1961.

Regardless, an Australian entrepreneur, Howard Lightburn saw the potential of the "everyman car." He approached Frisky's own Gordon Bedson to develop one for him. So, the Zeta Sports.

As we go down the line of mini and micro-cars, we will find there are many that are not frail or flimsy at all. Some, though small, do look quite solidly built. They should be. To be practical, they must be both safe, durable and provided with ample load-carrying capacity. So, it is not a good idea to go ultra small just for the sake of saving gas. A gas-efficient little car could be small, and yet be large enough to carry two people and their things.

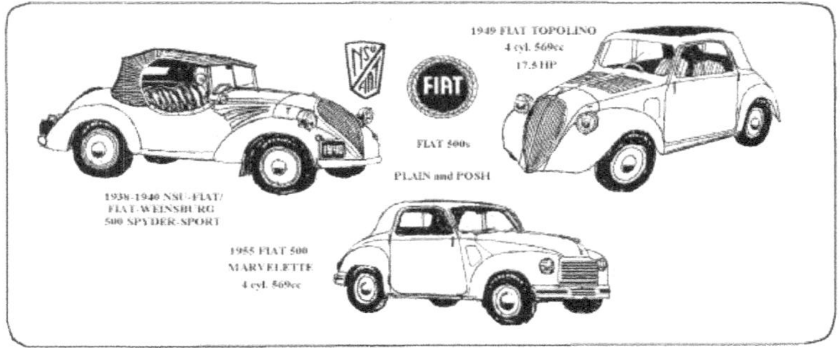

A good example is the FIAT 500 of the fifties. This mini family car came from a long line of little "mouse cars" the FIAT (Fabbrica Italiana Automobili Torino) works put out for the "hoi polio" of Italy. The FIAT 500's illustrious grand daddy was called "Topolino" or simply, "Little Mouse" in Italian. About 10 feet long, it was just-right for two people. The space back of the front bucket seats could accommodate two children although it was intended for luggage. Being basically a two-seater, therefore, the 4-cylinder 569cc engine was considered a big engine for it.

A much more practical car—the 600 replaced the Topolino in 1955. Designed around a box-shaped body, it was more spacious and could fit four people comfortably. Yet, it was lighter. With its larger engine of 633cc, it had plenty of go power, and many of them became tuners. The Abarth variants were especially potent. All repowered by larger engines of 747, 847 and 982cc, and able to exceed 100 MPH, they were true race cars.

All the same, blazing speed was not everybody's idea of hot performance. To a large percentage of the population during those austere times, gas mileage was. Everyone knew that FIAT, since it began making cars in 1899 had designed and produced as many, if not more large, luxurious and high-performance cars than many of its contemporaries. They knew also that FIAT was a leader in the design and development of the smallest of gas-sippers, and they were not about to let the FIAT top brass forget that. So, I am sure, the call for a new, and thriftier 500, to step into the shoes of the much beloved mouse went out, loud and clear, for a couple years later, in 1957, FIAT reopened its 500 production line.

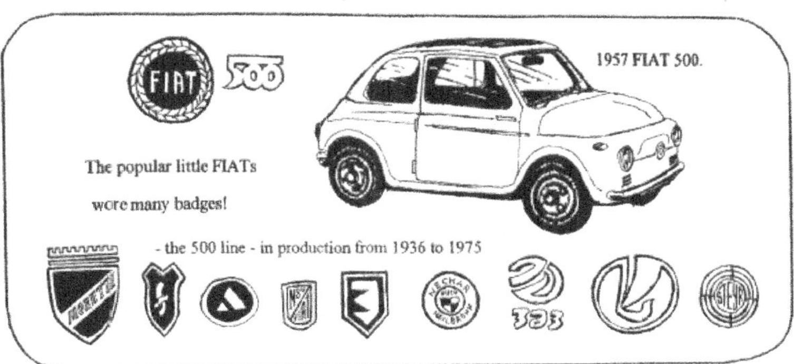

The new, or nuova 500 was an instant hit. Just about 10 feet in length, it clearly redefined the term "micro-car." The motoring public loved its modern, all-business, yet jaunty look. The fact that it could now seat four adults and a child made it even more "a keeper." It was rightly dubbed a "super-micro" when it won the Belgium to Slovenia and back Liege-Brescia-Liege Rally in 1958.

Enterprising carmakers everywhere, on the other hand were sold on how well engineered it was and made deals with FIAT to clone it under license. It did not take long before many little 500 look-a-likes or sound-a-likes were tooting and tooling all over Europe. The Italians called the new Cinquecentos, "Etceterinis," meaning, cars wearing the badges of so many other companies eager to base their own cars on the 500's excellent running parts to meet the expanding postwar market for cars of very low cost.

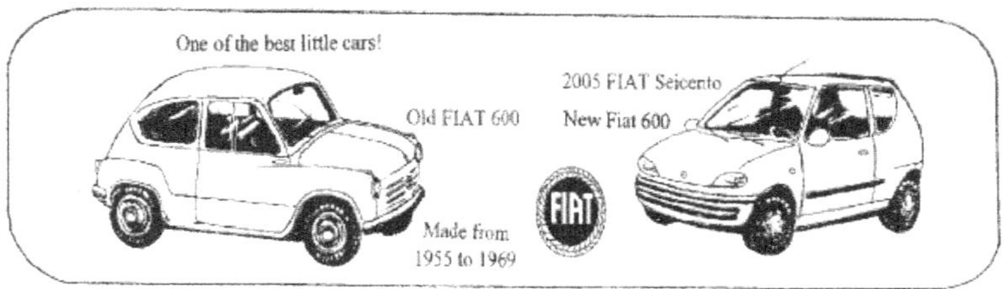

The 600, too will forever be remembered in the same way. It was a basic car with plenty of potential built into it. I saw how easy it was for one to pull its engine for a thorough bench overhaul. The car was that straightforward to service and soup up. There was no need to tear out the transmission first, or to completely dismantle the engine compartment just to get it out. The 633cc four-cylinder engine was even light enough for two to lift by hand.

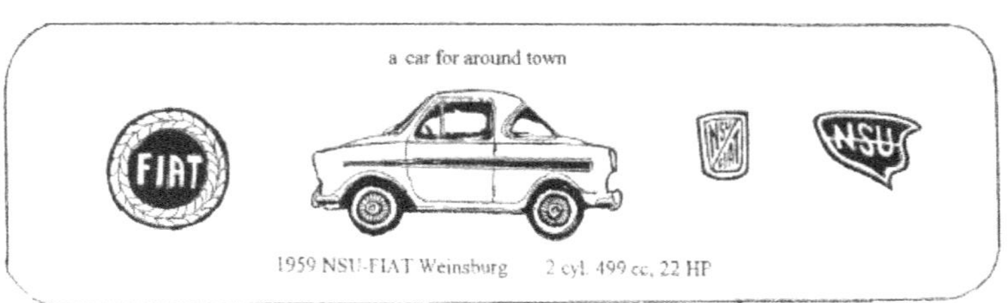

Germany's Neckar-Sulm or NSU was one company that used both the FIAT 500s and 600s as platforms for its deluxe little cars. I will show you more of them later. Steyr-Puch of Austria too did the same. Abarth, Italy's biggest builder and racer of tuner FIATs fielded a whole stable of the most successful high performance

500s and 600s, ever. Its name is, even today, synonymous with speed and performance—in a small package. Let me quote a few lines from an article that came out in the April 17, 1959 issue of the Autocar. They will give you a sense of how potent these FIAT Abarths were at the Monza 12-hours that year. "The 750cc Gran Turismo class was of course, the fastest and most interesting class, all cars being Abarth-FIAT-Zagato machines, and no fewer than nine were of the new, fast twin-overheadcamshaft type. These little cars reached speeds in the region of 112 MPH.... The small Abarth 750cc after its Sebring debut proved in top form." That is top-flight technology.

For the record, I will list the car makers that used the little FIATs as a platform for their own line of specialty cars in the 50s and 60s: Abarth, Autobianchina, Ghia, Giannini, Lombardi, Moretti, Steyr-Puch, Vignale, NSU-Weinsburg, and Zagato. A perfect 10. Can you name a car built here that can better that?

By the way, we recently saw GM put the brakes on its Oldsmobile line. Lest it be forgotten, this illustrious make, was launched by Ransome E. Olds in 1897—way, way before Chevy, Cadillac, Pontiac, Buick, and many other carmakers here. And if you guessed the REO trucks were built by R.E. Olds, you guessed right. I have always loved the 88s and 98s and I was sorry to see this grand old American nameplate get taken down. The Oldsmobile Holidays and Futuramics were all beautiful and worth developing.

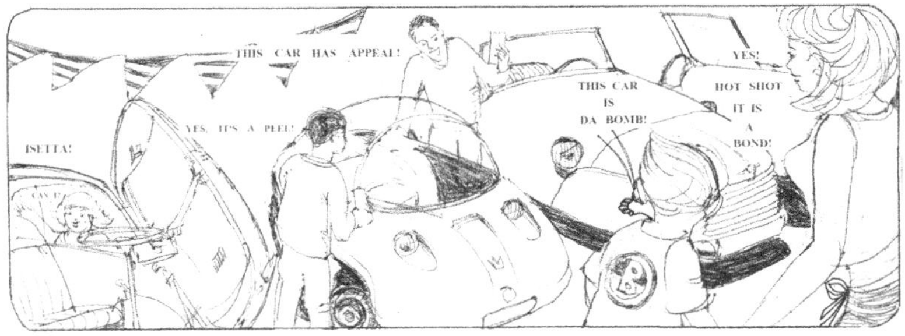

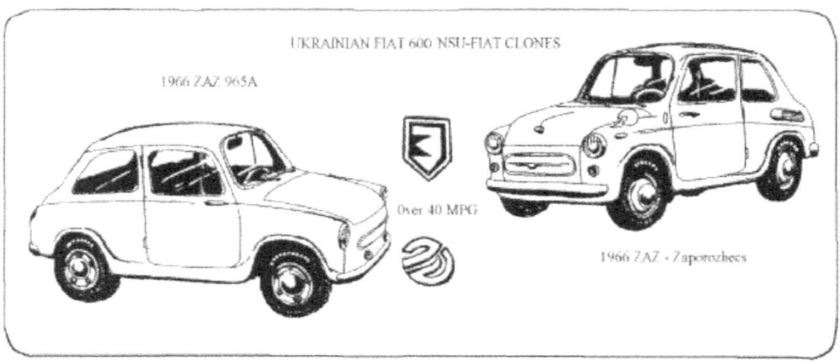

The ZAZs (Zaporozhskiy Avtomobilnyi Zavod) and Yaltas of Russia and also the ZAZs of Ukraine were NSU and FIAT 600 derivatives. As they say, "one good turn deserves another," and the tough little FIATs got their turn when they were in Russia to go everywhere, and to where roads, often no more than tracks, led everywhere and nowhere. The latter referring to the many outlying villages in the interminable steppes settled by yurt-dwellers and yak herders. The little ZAZs might be prone to rust, but their stout little hearts did beat in time with those who simply wanted solid transportation value. Some of these cars, from what I have learned, have been brought stateside by collectors. In Europe, good examples go for around 5000 Euros, or about US$5500.

In 1972, the FIAT 500 was replaced by the 126. It flaunted the classic angular look of the time. The engine size was increased progressively from 574cc, and after some upgrading, a 704cc power unit that put out 26 HP was available for this little car which was as light and small as its predecessor. Imagine the potential for it! In continuous production for ten years, the 126 proved its worth though it never quite equaled the original "nouva" 500.

The Seicento, FIAT's new 600, was introduced in 2005. I am sure it was so named to honor the original 600 which came on the motoring scene in 1955, fifty years earlier, and proved to the world that a little family car can be both mild and wild.

With a 900cc engine, the Seicento will certainly keep alive the spirit of one of the world's greatest minis, for a long time. I can see a great many being turned into tuners in the years ahead. Who is to say that it will not become another icon of the automotive world, and be remembered with cars like the Austin/Morris Mini, the Citroen 2CV, the old Beetles and the first Seicento?

Moretti was one company we listed earlier on that also sought to make what FIAT manufactured—even better. It catered to those who would be willing to pay a premium for something more luxuriously appointed. The 1966 Moretti 595 SS, most representative of the company's mini-car line, gave the sports car crowd a classy little speedster with FIAT mechanics that was both reliable and easy to maintain.

The Autobianchina company offered mini FIAT 500-based station wagons and business vans in addition to their cute two-seater micro runabouts. Its little sporty cabriolets were especially attractive. Picture the Dueposti topless. What a sweet thang! The sweeter too, being that it was not just for play. This car was totally practical in both the city and country. Founded in 1955, Autobianchina combined the talents of FIAT, Pirelli and Bianchina. It became part of FIAT in 1967. Lancia, another famous Italian marque took this specialty car company over in 1969.

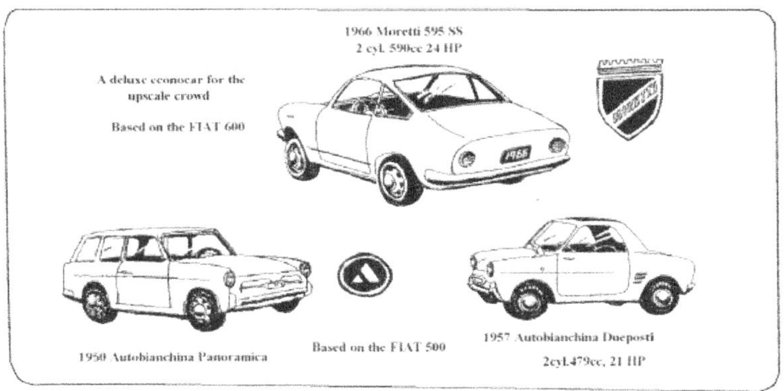

Enrico Piaggio, an Italian aircraft and engine designer was the man behind the little Vespa 400. Interestingly, he had his little personal two-seater built in France. (One source said that he did that to avoid getting his 400s into a turf war with the hugely popular FIAT 500s.) Already famous for his Vespa scooters, he hoped to develop his tiny cars for those Vespa owners who were looking to move up to something nicer. Or gutsier? (Vespa 400s were raced in the famous Liege-Brescia-Liege Rally for under 1000cc cars too!) Had he pressed on, I am sure, he would still be making the 400 today. It had all the basic features of a winner: a tested and guaranteed fuel-efficient rear engine coupled to a rugged rear-drive in the classic micro-car configuration—perfect for two people interested in just getting from A to B with the least fuss and expense.

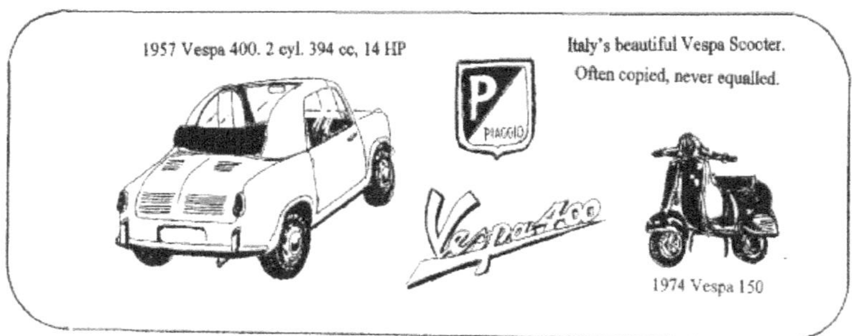

Although the 400 is no longer made, Piaggio is still doing wonderful today manufacturing all kinds of "scootabouts" for the thrifty crowd all over the world. Recently, I saw one of their two-passenger three-wheelers in a scooter dealership. Although well-built, and quite pretty, it was tiny. Powered by only a 49cc engine, it was intended strictly for city use.

Another interesting micro-car from Italy was the 1954 Panther 400. It was powered by a two-cylinder diesel engine of 520cc displacement. Pretty adequate for a car just 11 feet long. Exhaust emissions from this micro would be a non-issue. With so many small displacement diesel engines coming into wide use today, (and you will soon see that when we get to the corral where the latest micro-cars are displayed,) I would say that the Panther could be lauded as a trend-setter being that it was produced over fifty years ago.

Now, lets go over to that hummock, our "French Quarter,"where are gathered many cars from France. The several interesting makes from there have been a source of much fascination to me, even though we have not had much luck with French cars here in America. We "gas-and-go" types do not understand cars the way our French cousins do is why, I think. While they coddle their cars, having gone through all the birth pangs after the birth of the automobile and yeah, suffered through the years of its growing pains since the late 1800s when Peugeot, Panhard, Renault and Citroen came on the scene with their respective wheeled creations, we regard our cars as mere conveyances. A "utility vehicle" by definition. So, from the earliest years, our cars were built to take hard use and abuse. And to be as maintenance-free as possible. So, the "Detroit Iron" moniker. A direct result of this is our total dislike of any car that is needy of care or feeding. We expect our cars to run. Even without oil, it seems! And we simply trade them in, or we dispose of them when they break.

This "who gives a damn, it's only a car" attitude, by and large has yet to take hold in the Old Country. Thankfully. To many there, a car is still much like a toy for pops. Cleverly crafted by a Geppetto for grown kids to fuss over. Too special to be taken casually and too expensive to be abused or treated like a disposable piece of "you know what." Just something stamped out of cold steel and rolled off a mass-production line by faceless robots. I can still remember when the trusty old VW Beetle's durability was jokingly attributed to its having been made by elves in the Black Forest. Or, when an old Porsche Speedster's uneven running was with a shrug of the shoulders, blamed on its lack of exercise. There is something about cars made in Europe!

Talking about VWs, our Beetle shown here is prove positive that it is not HP or MPH that makes a car "hot." It is not its looks either. What makes a car a good car is how it runs. This car did that well, although it was not perfect. Its heater was weak and needed improving. Designed by the famous Dr. Ferry Porsche and made originally in 1938 as Hitler's "KdF wagen," or "Kraft durch Freude wagen," which translated means "Strength through Joy wagon," it was produced for over four decades. A copy of the then rather futuristic Czechoslovakian Tatra, it went through just minor changes throughout its long history. That the car sold a million a year in the sixties despite its fifties style must tell us that it had a timeless quality about it. Built so solid it could float, one was actually outfitted with a propeller and "motor-boated" from the Isle of Man to County Cumbria in 1973. Another made it across the Straits of Messina faster than the local ferry! Read more about it in media.vw.com. This and other interesting facts regarding the many makes of car shown here can be verified on the Internet.

"A true water Beetle fever raged in 1973, after the body of the Beetle proved to be seaworthy during several swimming attempts that ended happily. In Italy, a man mastered the Straits of Messina between Calabria and Sicily with his VW 1200 which had been carefully sealed and fitted with a propeller...
Afterwards the Viking, Malc Buchanan set off in the very rough waters of the Irish Sea. Starting from the Isle of Man he reached the county of Cumbria in England after seven and a half hour afloat. " <media.vw.com>

The old Beetle was tough too. Summer or winter, it could be pushed to the max on the freeway or off. The Germans found they could drive their "People's Car" at 68 MPH on the Autobahn all day. There were no worries regarding coolant leaks, let alone boilovers or freeze-ups as it was air-cooled. With the weight of its rear engine over its drive wheels, its traction in the snow was something.

Then, as its outward shape stayed basically the same, year after year, it needed no retooling, and so its price could be kept low. For the $1500 it cost in the sixties, it gave back times more in owner satisfaction dividends. So, with over 21 million sold, the Beetle, or Kever in Europe, certainly deserves a spot in our show. It has my applause although it gave just average gas mileage.

Another Volkswagen we must not forget is the sharp looking Golf. Introduced in 1974 when sales of the aging Beetle were starting to flag, it sold over 22 million in eight years. That record should tell our troubled car makers here how to go about saving themselves.

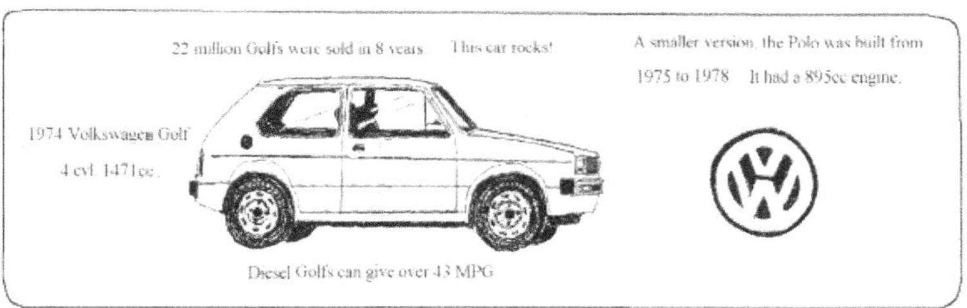

The original Mini too, gets my vote. Designed by Sir Alec Issigonis to deal a knockout blow to all the "dreadful bubble cars," as he called them, the Mini proved itself up to the task. It was more substantial than the other little cars it went up against, but like the Beetle, it was no looker. It was just—cute, in its own way. Referred to as the "shoebox car" the first models were really bare-bones, with crude pull-cable door release, and sliding glass windows. But as they say, "beauty is only skin deep," and in the case of the Mini the beauty of its heart and soul was what sold all five million of them over a ten-year production run. The demand was so great for it that Innocenti of Italy helped crank them out for a while. Even the Queen of England bought one.

One of the most interesting cars has to be the Citroen 2CV. Love it for its engineering, or hate it for its quirky looks, it is (still) the only car, we are told that could be purchased, and driven clear across the Sahara without much preparation. Since 1949, the year it was made, the 2CV, which stands for "Deux Chevaux," or "Two Horses" has been both lauded and ridiculed. Many think it is "butt-ugly." And arguably, it is. So much so that it has been called the "Ugly Duckling" in all Europe. But here, ugly is only skin-deep, and if one would care to look at this car closely, one would find pure engineering genius. Together with the VW Beetle, it has proved to us that style is not all there is, with all the clever design touches with their crisp, criss-crossing cut-ins. Rather it is the "can-do" spirit that its engineers have built into it. How many of our cars have that?

Andre Citroen created the 2CV basically for the French farmers who sorely needed a small family truck that could carry their goods, and especially their daily load of eggs across the rutty fields without breaking any of them. They got what they wanted in the 2CV for its novel front-rear shared suspension system gave it a truly compliant ride while the thrifty two-cylinder engine was as stout as it came. So well did the 2CV turn out that variants were available with two engines for die-hard adventurers to take to the ends of the earth. Though it was offered with one color: mouse-grey for the longest time, it was produced for some 31 years.

Car-buyers who wanted a better looking 2CV had a choice for a time in the Bijou. Built in England for the upscale and more conservative British market, it sold, but not as well as the original. So, in time, it got dropped, leaving the 2CV to soldier on. Quite unfortunate, for the Bijou sported one of the best body lines. Well balanced and harmoniously done, it had all the points of a winner. Probably it did poorly because of market conditions and timing, but be that as it may, I share the same opinion with many about the 2CV in that "if it ain't broken, don't fix it." Keep the 2CV going. Give it time to prove its worth. That it worked well will make it beautiful.

The much larger Citroen 11 CV worked well too, and I can say that there is not a car in its class that can match it. So, I must tarry awhile to recount my time behind the wheel of this antique "Traction Avant," or front-wheel drive family sedan. Long and low-slung, this smooth oldie was what gave me such a rush when I took it out on the road some years ago. I shall never forget the thrill of it. What a trip, just to see its long hood sweep across the landscape, with its two large gleaming round headlamps leading the way as I negotiated each curve that came up ahead. So quick around corners it was too! Its windshield could be cranked open for that "wind-in-your-face" experience as you worked its shifter which stuck out from the dashboard.

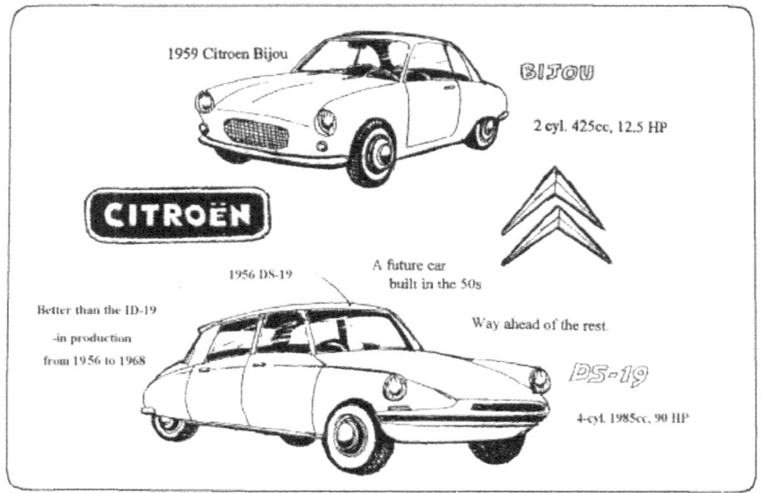

The big but more modern DS-19 was equally special, and therefore, scores a quick comment here. Though it debuted in the fifties and showed what cars in the future would be like, it still turns heads today. Why, we have here, a car that was already way ahead of its time when it first came out.

Its active hydro-pneumatic suspension system gave it the ability to glide over the worst bumps and clear the deepest ruts with ease as its ride height could be increased to a full 13 inches on the fly. The ultra-streamlined profile spoke French, fluently. One would be hard put to improve on it. The spare tire location itself, in front of the engine and radiator, was proof positive, that the layout of this car was thought out with great care. Granted there were areas that could have been improved upon, but this car to my mind, stood head and shoulders above many others, then and now.

Despite a long and productive life of almost 100 years, Citroen fell on hard times, and was bought up by rival Peugeot in 1976. As part of the Peugeot Group, its double helix trademark lives on, and continues to point the way—up.

The French Renault 4CVs, like the Citroen 2CVs were interesting. In many ways, they mirrored their illustrious founders. Read about the histories of these visionaries and you will see what I mean. Both Andre Citroen and the Renault brothers lived in times when great cars were built by men of conviction and stature. When cars were the products of great minds, and not some cunningly conceived corporate money-grubbing scheme.

The fifties and the sixties were, therefore, truly the halcyon days of the automobile. Look at the many cars from that period that are much sought after by collectors today. They have that magic and mystique about them that the modern cars we see out on the road lack. No mistake about it. Compared, most of today's cars are basically just shameless copies of one model or another. Be they hatchbacks or notch backs, they are all hard to tell apart from afar. So absolutely lacking in "car-risma" are they! Tell me if this year's Volvos have not lost its "solid Swede" appeal by going the way of all flash and adopting without restraint, what is trendy in its body style. Or why is it that SAABs and Subarus have suddenly melded?

Well, here is one little car that will forever stand out. Called the 4CV because it had four doors, was powered by a little four-cylinder gas engine and could seat four people. Clever, and how! Leave it to the French! A walk around will show the compactness of this family car Renault introduced to the world in 1947. It could be said to be both small and large at the same time, meaning, it could easily pack four adults into its tiny passenger compartment like a regular car. With its four doors, it was easy to get in and out of. Although power was provided by a four-cylinder engine, its gas mileage was as good as any mini. Being that its engine was mounted in the rear, usable luggage space was provided under the hood up front. The car turned out to be a great success and so it remained in production for almost 20 years. A total of over 8 million were made. Even Hino (now a part of Toyota) was once upon a time, licensed to build it for the Japanese market. To the delight of all who know and love this little car, a retro 4CV was unveiled at a recent car show.

Renault was founded in 1889 and made everything from tractors to tanks. You name it, Renault made it. Aircraft engines, marine engines, buses, trucks... Being the world's sixth largest automaker, it must have had an iron in every fire. To its credit, it even reached over here to help AMC, (American Motors Corp—the outfit that built the Ramblers, and which eventually brought us the Hummers) get through some tough times in the late seventies. Thus, several cars Renault manufactured were, by agreement, sold here as AMC Eagles. In return, a whole line of the medium and large AMC Rambler Classics, Rebels, and Ambassadors that were shipped over to France were re-badged as Renault Ramblers. The deal did not go as well as anticipated, but Renault stayed strong. So much so that this dynamite company is even reaching out to help poor GM today!

Would you know too, that back in the mid sixties, Renault was the first auto giant to introduce a subcompact with revolutionary race-car type disc brakes on all four wheels into the US market? That car was the rather boxy and not at all sporty R-10! Go figure. Then, in 1972, it pushed its tiny R-5 as "Le Car" to drive, if you needed something that was excellent on gas. The Renault 5 went head-to-head with the young upstart Honda Z600. Although it lost out stateside, it remained in production some thirteen years in Europe. Much longer than the Honda. So, despite the many horror stories by these so-called auto experts here, it must not have been too bad.

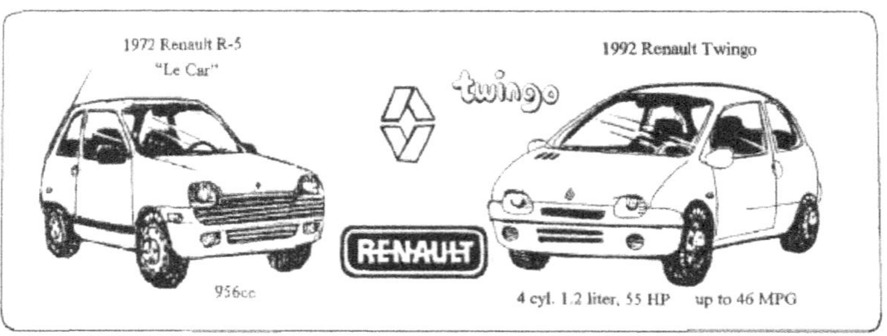

If you do not agree, you have your reasons and I respect them. There are indeed many here in America that did not have much luck with what the French made. Be that as it may, I would like to submit to you that it was our "power everything" and "muscles for brains" style of driving that did in cars like the Renaults, Citroens, and Peugeots. (Or for that matter, the MGs, Triumphs, Alfas, and FIATs.) Had we gone by the book to break them in right, been more careful about their feeding, and taken it upon ourselves to not heavy-handedly bully, bend or break them the way we do our beasts, we would have done well with them.

In this millennium, Renault, together with Nissan and Mack trucks, has forged ahead with the introduction of many new products in Europe. Their super economical car lines have gone big time. From the 1.2 to the 3.5-liter models, I counted no less that 130 different types in the current listing. The gas-sipper 1.2s number over 15 models priced from 9,345 to 15,545 Euros. (Ford is second in line over in Europe with 112.) It would be impossible for me to include all the latest 1 .2s here at the show—as it is really about the older minis and micros. However, I will do one that is quite representative of Renault's current offerings—the Twingo. The smallest, the "Authentique," sells for 9,345 Euros, which is about USD$ 12,000.

Without a doubt, carmakers in the Old Country, unlike the ones here have kept pace with the times. Having been through two world wars, and numerous oil shocks, they know that there will always be a need for fuel-efficient cars. Is not experience the best teacher? So, the many minis and micros that are still rolling off the production lines together with the super roadsters and deluxe limousines there. Our Big Three, here, on the other hand, seem, kind of clueless and one-tracked, in comparison. Stuck in the "big is better" rut, they are trying forever to convince us that we need hundreds and hundreds of horses to get us from one side of town to another. Or to be more exact, from one gas station to another. If that is a bother, they will go ahead and just give us a larger gas tank.

Once upon a time, looks used to be "it." Cars were heavy on chrome and two-tone paint. Low was in style. Now, the jingle is that we need a truck that can climb Mount Everest or cross the trackless Sahara to take us to work. Or one with enough ground clearance to ford a small river to bring home the groceries. Ah, what to drive—in today's concrete jungle!

Well, if all that patter does not point to the young, and (still-wet-behind-the-ears) restless among us, what does? The US strikes me as being quite like that ,an over-grown city kid, compared with say, a much older and more knowledgeable country cousin, like Holland.

Yes, Holland, or The Netherlands, the low country sandwiched between Germany and France must be one of the car-craziest! And I am not basing my statement on the disproportionate number of car clubs there alone. If you want to know, Holland is home not only to Spyker, an aero-engine maker, and pioneer car-builder of renown founded in 1898, but also to hundreds of little automotive enterprises down through the decades. It would take many pages just to touch on all the 200 plus companies that Jan Lammerse's "Autodesign in Nederland" listed. Truly, the Dutch can be justly proud of their contributions to the world of the automobile.

First, a little "Ripley" for you. Believe it or not, Nijmegen, one of Holland's principle cities recently celebrated its 2000th birthday! And we thought Miss Liberty was old when she pushed 200. But don't let the numbers fool you. At age 2000, this lofty city, and all of Holland, I must not forget to include, look as modern as today. Much more than many of our cities do, at 200 something. And times more than many others in Europe. Or Asia. Take a trip there when you have the time and you will be amazed at how vibrant this little powerhouse of a country is. Though just a little larger than the state of Maryland, Holland is the big guy on many of the world's stages. Recently, Volvo's ocean racers came to town, and guess what, the top two sails bore Dutch logos. Impressive! Why? Here is a yachting event that was pioneered by the Dutch back in the 17th Century, and the Dutch are still very much the masters at ruling the waves today. What can I say but that they are doers, not idle talkers, having ventured outside of the box? For your info, even the word "yacht" is of Dutch origin.

Then, take a look at their windmills. And be amazed. From the day I saw one in action up close, I have been fascinated by wind-power. Even though that particular mill was put in operation for the benefit of tourists, its potential was plain to see. The sails, turned by the gentlest of breezes, were not even completely unfurled. Yet, their power seemed unstoppable. Useful work was being done, right before my very eyes. That day, I witnessed the harnessing of the cleanest form of energy—ever, by the ingenious Dutch. The many gears within it, all carved out of wood, and lined with metal, leisurely turning the millworks in the upper and lower floors were by themselves, a sight to behold. Although they seemed to whir away effortlessly, their tremendous driving force was clear to all. The heart-thumping pulse-beat of the levers working the pumps and turning the gearworks will stir anyone's soul! Experience all this and more by visiting Holland one summer. There is so much to see and do in this dynamic little country!

The dyke that windmill sat on was also a sight to behold. Though a good many year have flown since my visit there, I still remember how massive the earthen mound looked. It was surmounted by a regular roadway, stretching as far as eye could see. It held back the sea from the rustic landscape that sloped sharply away below the mill.

So, should not our engineers smarten up, and be building dykes instead of shoring up the levees around New Orleans to better protect it from the bigger hurricanes that are projected to hit the Gulf region soon? They should do like the Dutch master-builders, link the dykes up with the road system. All politics aside, the hurricane season will strike every year regardless of who rules the Big Easy. And we have been warned that worse storms are to come. Yet, few seem concerned. The fact that many of the displaced have returned to rebuild—on the same sinking sand tells me that hard lessons have not been learned. And that fools never differ. It is not unlike how we regard the coming oil shortage! Are we not, with each passing day, heading inexorably into another gas crisis at full speed? How soon to a $100 fill-up?

With a gallon of gas currently going for over US$6.00 now in Holland, one would think that their newly resurrected Spyker car company would be shelving their super-sized deluxe fire-breathers and be tooling up to build a line of thrifty autos for our present oil-addicted generation. They could call the new line of cars "Dutch" perhaps, in honor of the Brothers Van Doorne, makers of the old DAFs.

Why, the Dutch DAFs were, to my mind, some of the most innovative cars ever made. Called "the cars of a hundred gears," DAFs were all standard equipped with the revolutionary Variomatic transmission, the brainchild of Huub Van Doorne. With this belt-driven "shiftless" drive, one could go just as fast through the gears in forward or reverse. You flick the shifter between the two positions, that is all! This belt and pulley automatic worked so well that although DAF is no longer in the business of making cars today, Van Doorne's Transmissie B.V of Tilburg, The Netherlands, is still very busy, specializing in the production of its new "Transmatic." Back in 1999, one could order a Nissan Primera with it. Today, both the Saturn Vue and the Nissan Murano can be had with a similar option. A DAF Formula race car was once even outfitted with this continuously variable transmission, or CVT drive. It was however excluded from participating in the race because the judges ruled that the unit gave it an "unfair advantage." They must know why.

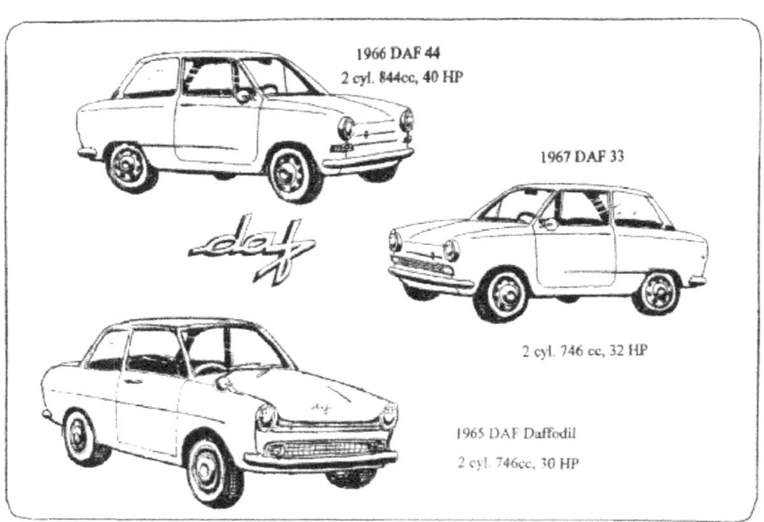

The smaller and lighter CVTs are currently utilized by the tiniest of scooters and micro-cars that are manufactured for the easy rider crowd. No shifting. Just forward and reverse. And step on it. What could be simpler? It is the future, as Huub saw it.

And truly farsighted he was! With over 90% of cars today sold with automatic transmission, I daresay it will not be long before everyone will come to see how much better it is to not have to be messing around with the gears. Anyone who has been caught in today's traffic tie-ups will be smiles ahead driving with full auto. Any engine and drivetrain too, may I add.

All this came about in 1949 when the Van Doorne's garage and machine shop modernized and became DAF: "Van Doorne's Aanhangen-fabriek." But after a year or so, working with trucks, buses and trailers, (aanhangen,) the two Van Doorne brothers, Huub and Wim decided to move up into automobiles, with the dream of making a car that was better than the FIAT Topolino, the Citroen 2CV, or the Renault 4CV. Therefore, the Van Doorne's Automobiel Fabriek, or DAF nameplate. Huub was inspired by his Buick Dynaflow's smooth hydramatic and sought to find a way to perfect a drive system that would be as good, and yet, light enough to fit into his new idea small car. He had a brainwave and hit on a system of drive belts and pulleys to select the most ideal gear ratio for any speed. So, the Variomatic!

Out of the many cars DAF made from 1958 to 1975, I have chosen only the smaller ones for the show. All were powered by two-cylinder engines. Their full line included beach-buggies, station-wagons, hatchbacks, family sedans, sporty coupes, pickups, mini-tractors that towed little trailers, army jeeps, and even specially designed and outfitted postal delivery vans for the Scandinavian markets. Whether powered by two or four-cylinder engines, they were all fuel-efficient. And tough. Their successful participation in the London-Sidney marathons should leave no doubt as to how well put together they were.

DAF trucks too have done great and were quite consistent rally winners, imagine that. For the record, they took the Paris-Dakar trophy in 1982, 1985 and 1987. They were the first trucks to go with turbo-diesel power too. In Europe, the DAF LF was voted "Truck of the Year" in 2002. That was a remarkable achievement, for Mercedes trucks have for generations been the big boys in the European trucking world.

In spite of its many accomplishments, DAF, the car company was sold to Volvo in 1975. While DAF continued making its line of full-size commercial trucks, buses, and tractors, Volvo made DAF passenger cars. The subcompact DAF-Volvo 66GL made from 1975 looked very much like a mini Volvo 142, right down to its broken badge-bar grille. It was because of that, that by 1981, Volvo stopped making them as their DAFs altogether.

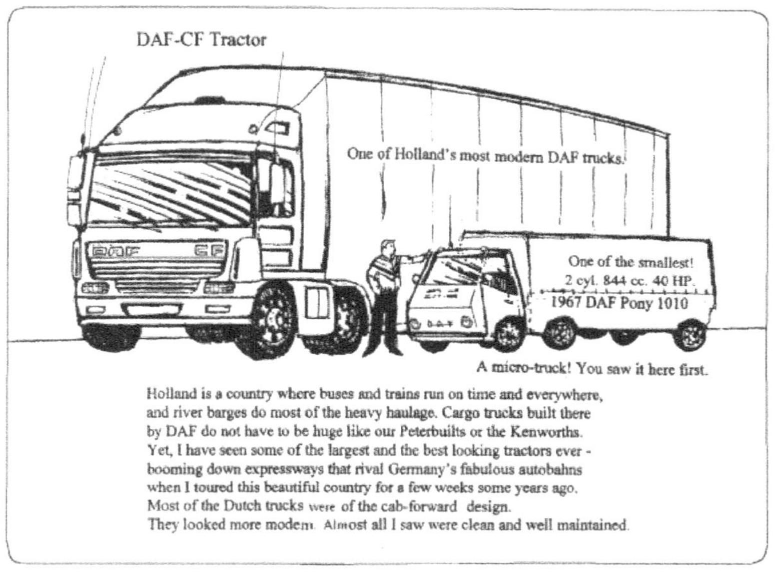

Holland is a country where buses and trains run on time and everywhere, and river barges do most of the heavy haulage. Cargo trucks built there by DAF do not have to be huge like our Peterbuilts or the Kenworths. Yet, I have seen some of the largest and the best looking tractors ever - booming down expressways that rival Germany's fabulous autobahns when I toured this beautiful country for a few weeks some years ago. Most of the Dutch trucks were of the cab-forward design. They looked more modern. Almost all I saw were clean and well maintained.

You may be wondering why DAF folded. For sure, it was not because its cars were bad. Although it was bandied about by not a few that DAFs were just too tame, and that they were really intended for the older folks, for they were so easy to drive, what really did it in was a combination of many factors. Market timing was certainly one. Stiff foreign competition was surely another. There were just too many good cars a Dutch citizen could pick from. Then, there were many who felt that the high-level shell game played in the boardroom by DAF and Volvo execs was what eventually closed down the car-making sector of this fine old marque.

Another interesting little car from Holland that we have here at the show was hand-made by a Puck Van Beekum. Called Citeria, it attracted much attention in 1958 when it ran very well at the Zandvoorste F-1 race circuit in Holland. Those indeed were the days when creativity ruled, and when many-a car-nut could doodle some new-fangled idea of a car on scratch paper, put it together in some back alley garage and track test it without having to fill out hundreds of emissions-related questions. Van Beekum's tiny fiber-bodied hot-rod was powered by the same twin-cylinder engine the BMW 600 had. It could go over 84 MPH with ease. It was a pity that for lack of adequate funding, this practical speedster was not further developed for mass production. With so much work put into its design and construction, Van Beekum should never have allowed the Citeria to be sidelined. I have been told that one professionally restored model of this cute little car is still shown by its proud owner in Holland.

Now, on to quite an old make—Goggomobil. Founded by Maurus Glas, in 1883, Hans Glas GmbH Maschinenfabrik must surely be one of the more interesting car companies in autodom. Why? Hans, one of Maurus' sons, was the one who, after he took over his father's agricultural machine company in 1952, built it up into one of Germany's great automobile manufacturing firms. Was I surprised to read about his having been here in America a good long time before he even thought to go into the car-making business. With the storm clouds of World War One gathering, his wise old dad thought it a good idea to send him here to work for Massey Ferguson, a well-known farm machinery manufacturer. It was not the best of times in America, then, as he soon found out, and so, he left, and went to Toronto, Canada. After the war, he came back and was hired as a production manager with our own Harley Davidson right here in Pennsylvania! Now, does that not get you wanting to know more about Goggomobils?

The Goggomobil company started up making scooters first. With the Italian Vespa scooters "Vespa-pa-pa-ing" away, (as their many commercials went,) in much of Europe and just about everywhere, Hans saw an opportunity and decided to get a piece of the action. He got down to design a scooter of his own. One that was more sturdier: an all-work-and-no-play kind of scoot-about. An original thinking man, he did not want a Vespa-look-alike. He was not one who was into any copycat kind of work anyway. So, his scooter was heavier, and much more manly. It reminded him of his favorite son Goggo. So, the name.

Hot after the Vespa, the BMW Isetta came on the scene, and it too went everywhere. Hans Glas decided to not be putt-putting around anymore, and it was not long before his micro-car project was underway. The car he came up with—the Goggomobil T-250, however was totally unlike the Isetta. It was a regular car, but only much smaller. Powered by an air-cooled 247cc rear engine in a basic three-box body style, it had space for four adults and their luggage. Over 40,000 of them were made. An interesting point about this car I found out is that it was the first to have an engine that used a timing belt. The T-300 came next in 1955. This workmanlike mini family car was more powerful, and a sporty cabriolet model was added to its line. Some, we have been told, found their way to the racetrack. In a recent issue of Classic Motor Monthly, there was an article that mentioned how a Goggomobil, driven by one Mr Coleby took the 350cc class record at Goodwood in the May of 1957.

The Glas Isar S35, a more deluxe micro that was also produced by Has Glas in 1960 looked very much like the Goggo T300 cabriolet. In fact, the Glas car line was geared to the upscale crowd, and the 1700s, 2600s and 3000s, all much larger than the T700 shown here were almost as big and long as the BMWs. All of them looked much like American-made cars too, with their modern grille-work, bright, beautiful paint jobs, and large, sharply raked windshields and generous window glass.

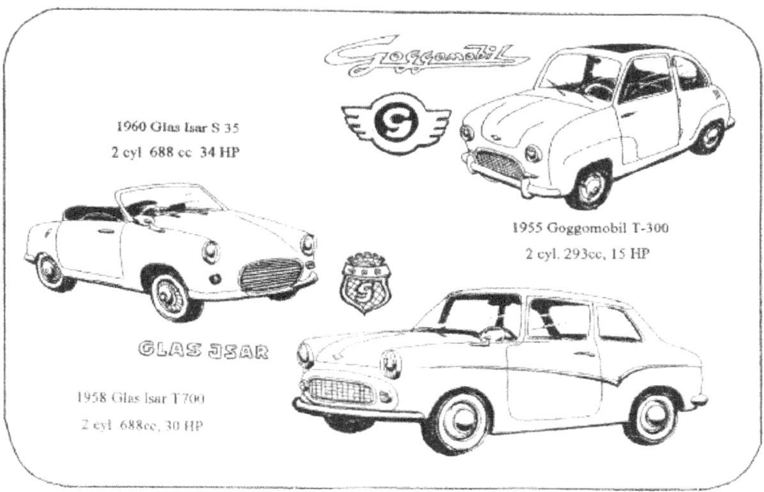

The little Goggos were also built under license in Spain. Some were even made down under—in Australia by Buckle Motors. They had redesigned bodies and were renamed the Dart. From what you see, the Dart's swoopy good looks must tell you right away that there was such a big difference between the German and Australian philosophies of style when it came to cars at that time. The Germans seemed to go for that practical and purposeful packaging, while the Australians preferred that sleek and low-slung race car look.

Another German make well-known throughout the world in the fifties and sixties was NSU. Named after the Neckar and Sulm, two rivers that passed near the plant, this company started life as a knitting machine factory. From the early 1900s, it branched out into bicycle production, and it was not long before it began to manufacture mopeds and motorcycles The superior quality of its products was apparent, for over a million of its mopeds were sold. Soon, cars followed, and within a few years, it was competing and winning in the European Grand Prix races. Its motorbikes were especially successful in the 1950 Isle of Man TTs.

To all the World War Two buffs out there, the crazy-looking Kettenkrad, a go-anywhere tracked motorcycle-like army personnel carrier the German Wehrmacht used everywhere was made by NSU.

It was after the cessation of hostilities that this very resilient company began to gear up and make "people-cars." It first joined hands with Italy's FIAT and manufactured a whole line of little cars based on the 500s, 600s and up. Its shapely and well-appointed Neckars were aimed squarely at the affluent. But it was the little Sports Prinz of 1958 that put NSU on the map. A more family-friendly variant, the Prinz III was added to the line in 1960, and over 9500 of them were sold. In 1961, the design was given the tubby American Chevrolet Corvair-look to make it roomier. The Sports Prinz remained the most well-received, and so, a special Wankel-powered Spider version was built from 1964 to 1967. It was a daring and dynamic move, for its new technology rotary was still being developed. All the same, this made the Spider one of the most collectible little cars. Excellent examples can fetch upwards of US$15,000 in the classic car market today That is twice that of its other mini-cars, and more than its larger Wankel powered sibling, the RO 80.

NSU became a part of Auto Union in 1932, pooling its resources together with Audi, Horch, DKW and Wanderer, the other four grand old German car makers. The group was taken over by Volkswagen in 1969. The NSU factory in Neckar-Sulm, continues to this day as a plant producing Audis.

If you thought that DKW made only motorcycles, let me show you a couple of their cars. But first, a little about the company a Danish engineer by the name of Jorgen Rasmussen founded in 1916. The original intent was to build a small steam powered car. So, the DKW nameplate which came from "Dampf Kraft Wagen," German for "steam powered vehicle." But as it turned out three years later, he succeeded with a little gas engine. It worked so well that he called it "Das Klein Wunder." So, DKW stayed DKW. Perfect.

That could also be said of the engine DKW made, for it was that good. Adapted to power many cars—SAABs, Trabants, Peels, among them in the fifties, its production life span was a remarkable 70 plus years. So successful was DKW that by 1928, when it was already touted as the largest motorcycle manufacturer in the world, it was able to move up quickly into car production. In 1931, it developed the front-wheel-drive concept for its cars, and under the direction of Dr. Porsche, DKW cars were setting all kinds of sales records. The next year, it joined forces with Horch and Wanderer to form Auto Union. The combined talents of the three companies resulted in many Grand Prix race records. We see its famous four-ring logos on the Audis of today.

Two of DKW's most beautiful mini-cars, the Junior and the SP Roadsters were built to look like scaled-down versions of classic American Fords to me. According to the Dutch classic car annual, "De Onschatbare Klassieker," DKW's SP Roadster, the mini T-Bird, in tip-top shape could command at least US$35,000 in the classic used car market.

So, I say, Audi should bring back the SP Roadster like Ford did with its T-Bird. The thrifty SP would do much better than Ford's retro, I am sure. Being powered by a three-cylinder 981cc engine, this high-style gas sipper would be just right for the times. With a little nip and tuck, this sleek little roadster could be a true fashion plate for other car companies looking to break away from the European tail-less, cut-back look.

Okay, since we know that the early SAABs were powered by DKW engines, let us take a look at the SAAB 92.

SAAB—Sweden's Svenska Aeroplan Aktiebolaget was founded in 1937 to build airplanes. Its cars came much later. So, the logo of a twin-engine airplane with propellers buzzing head-on. It's first car was hand-built in 1947 by some seventeen Swedish aeronautical engineers, and it was said that only one of them had a driver's license! I am sure he was the test pilot. Whatever, he and his crew did a great job building the prototype. Patterned around an airfoil, it was both strong and rigid. I call it the original smart car, for so much thought was put into its shape alone. Aerodynamically refined, being wind-tunnel tested, it could do 60 MPH on just 25 HP. That was something, for the car weighed a ton. Easily double that of any mini or micro-car. Like an airplane, it was overbuilt. And like a camouflaged fighter plane, it came only in one color—bottle-green.

SAAB made great little cars. A 1949 SAAB 92, if in excellent condition could be sold for over US$20,000 in the classic car market today. This smaller two-cylinder model was in continuous production until 1953. The more powerful 92Bs came next and were built until 1956. Although they looked kind of large, all of them were shorter in length than the VW Beetle.

The 93s were often raced in the European 750cc Touring Category. According to a report in the April 1959 issue of The Autocar, one came in first in its class at the 1959 Monza 12 Hours, winning over many souped-up FIAT 600s. It covered more than 908 miles at an average speed of 75.68 MPH. Quite a feat, for the little 748cc two-stroke engine would have to be turning at over 4,000 RPM for a better part of the 12-hour race! Take a moment to imagine yourself driving with the tachometer that wound up for an hour on the freeway and you will quickly get the picture. Now, add to the scene swarms of other cars doing the same for effect.

We have two micro-cars made right here in America next. Yes, we were once upon a time, into the simple life—as you can see, in how the two King Midgets in the show were made. It might look like a bucket of bolts, but the Model III was billed as "the world's #1 fun car," and it stayed in production for a good number of years after it came out in 1951. The company, King Midget was started by two Civil Air Patrol pilots, Claud Dry and Dale Orcutt in 1946. They were two very innovative guys, for they designed the Midget with its own unique automatic transmission and even made it possible for buyers to opt for the kit version. Had they continued to fine tune their car every year, all through the 25 years the company was in operation, they could very well be still making them today. In this great big country of ours, there is room enough for all types of automobiles, and with what we are getting charged at the gas pumps and service stations, surely room for cars like the "DIY," or "Do-It-Yourself" Midget.

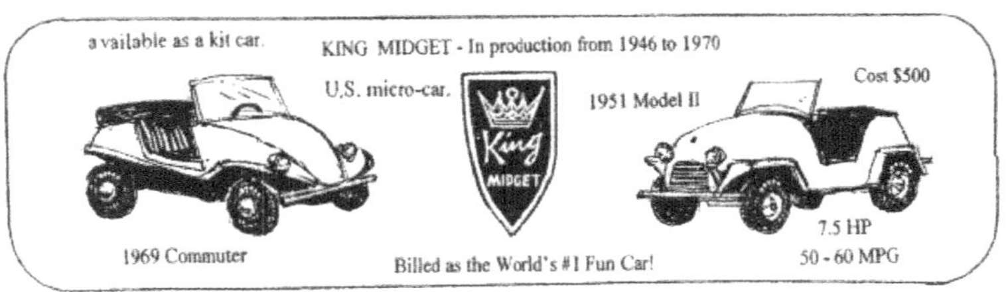

Although the company closed in 1970, a year after they rolled out the Commuter, King Midgets are still very much alive. Many have been restored and many are being shown by its club members all though the United States. There is a close-knit community of people who love these bare-bones micro-cars. That they were made here is one reason why they are special to them.

Another old US make that many regarded as "mini" was the Crosley. It was rather popular in the fifties, and many of them were modified for racing. I thought their little wood-paneled wagon to be somewhat dowdy looking though. But that is another story.

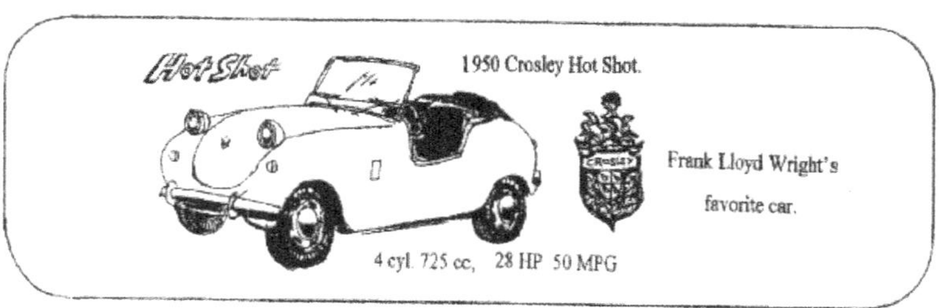

The Crosley Company, interestingly was known more for the part it played in World War Two. It manufactured the proximity fuzes that made it possible for the Allies to shoot down the German V-1 Buzz Bomb over London. General Patton himself credited the Crosley fuze for helping win the Battle of the Bulge. There, does that not make you want to learn more about the man behind the little Crosley cars—Powell Crosley Jr? This totally down-to-earth inventor was also the one who gave us the refrigerator door shelves, fancy that! Yet, he regarded his small car line the best, over and above all this other achievements, which included this world famous radio show and electronics products.

The German Lloyds too were that, although many thought them to be boring little cars. Too old fashioned. But they worked well. And they worked hard. You knew it when they were on the road. Their little engines did not let you forget that. They were quite loud.

Not to be confused with another Lloyd, a small four-seat car built by one Richard Lloyd of Lincolnshire, England, in 1936, the German Lloyd was part of the NAMAG (Norddeutsche Automobil und Motoren) automotive group of companies that were based in Bremen. In the early part of 1900, the cars they built were large, and powered by engines of 2.3, 3.6 and 5.5 liters.

It was not until they merged with the Hansa group, builders of the Goliath and Hansa line of cars, vans, micro-buses and trucks in 1950 and became Lloyd Motoren Werke that it started putting out the smaller and more sensible passenger cars. The Borgward arm of the company was the driving force that brought out the little 293 cc, two-cylinder Lloyd LC 300. This neat looking micro-car was followed by the 600. Called the Alexander, it was the best of the 600cc models. An ultra compact two-door family sedan, it could seat four people comfortably. Always into what was practical, Lloyd car company also built kombis, or station-wagons and vans. Although Lloyds were often the least costly vehicles in the automotive marketplace, they were placed third, after Opel and Volkswagen in reliability. So, I was not surprised at all when I read that one of their tough little boxer engines eventually became the model for what Subaru developed for its cars. A recent special classic car journal had an article about that. I found that most interesting. See how far the Subaru Car Company has come.

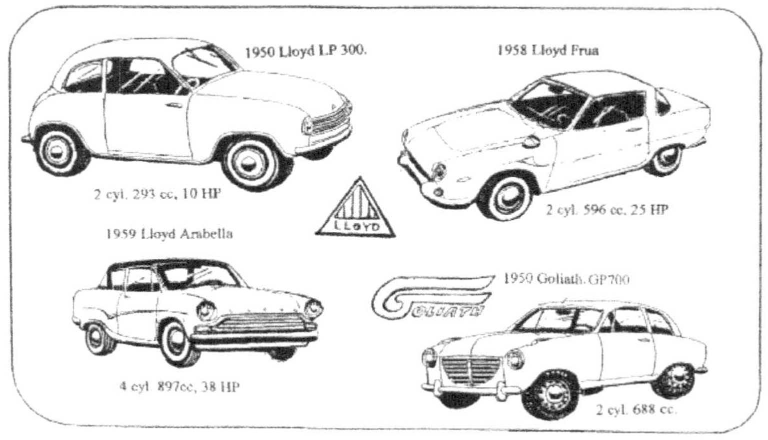

The Frua and Arabella came later in 1958 and 1959, respectively. Both were larger and even better appointed. The company was hoping to attract the younger and more affluent crowds with these two cars, I bet. Both were smaller than the Beetle, but you could never tell by looking at the drawings here. Their lines were that well-balanced. Unfortunately, when Borgward folded, due to circumstances beyond its control, Lloyd was forced to quit making automobiles altogether.

Had BMW gone the extra mile to help Borgward, this fine German marque might still be here with us today. But that is another story. If you were to google Borgward, you would get the picture.

BMW, Bayersiche Motoren Werke, or Bavarian Motor Works, founded in 1913, was one of the most successful German manufacturers of motorcycles and cars. As it had established itself as one of Germany's top engine designer and manufacturer even before World War Two, it was responsible for the development of high-performance aircraft engines for Hitler's Luthwaffe. Therefore, its production facilities were targeted for destruction by Allied bombers. Even so, it was able to pull itself out of the bombed-out belly of its factories after the hostilities ended and regroup. Though it took awhile for things to get sorted out, BMW pressed on. For some time, it kept itself going by making kitchen and farm equipment. Then, in 1954, when it was given the nod to restart its auto-making operations, it rolled out its first postwar car—the big and powerful 501 (See page 3). We know it to be one of their best products today. But in those austere times, it was just too much car for a Germany that was divided four ways, and suffering the setbacks brought about by war. The car cost three times the annual salary of an average worker then, and so, it did not sell. BMW therefore had to down-shift and keep on trucking, while it looked around for a money-maker.

Not far across the border, Italy's Isomoto was buzzing. This refrigerator company had also shifted gears to make something it could sell, and it had struck pay dirt. Its creation, the Isetta bubble car was so well received by the public that the production line could not keep up with the demand for it. BMW found an opportunity right there. The rest was, as they say, history.

Licensed by Iso to build its bubble car, BMW promptly put its well-respected "spinning propeller badge" on the humble, plainly apologetic-looking Isetta 300 and elevated it to star status. It became an international hit. The rather ungainly looking little car even competed in the famous Mille Miglia, a 1000-mile endurance race, in 1955, finishing in 267th place out of a field of 281 little cars. Picture if you will the scenario—with our little "rolling egg," (as it had come to be so fondly called,) fighting off the herds of bellowing FIATs which were the favorites of a great number of race fans. It put up a good show, just keeping itself from being run over all day. With its one banger of 250cc, in full cry the whole way, the odd little car must have stolen the show. Its tough, tenacious spirit won many hearts that day. It was not long before the 300 became the launching off point for BMW's own mini gas-saver—the 600 in 1957. Stretched and powered by a two-cylinder engine of 586cc, it kept the same nose of the 300 and added a second row of seat to accommodate two more adults in back. Although a great idea, it was never as popular as its smaller sibling.

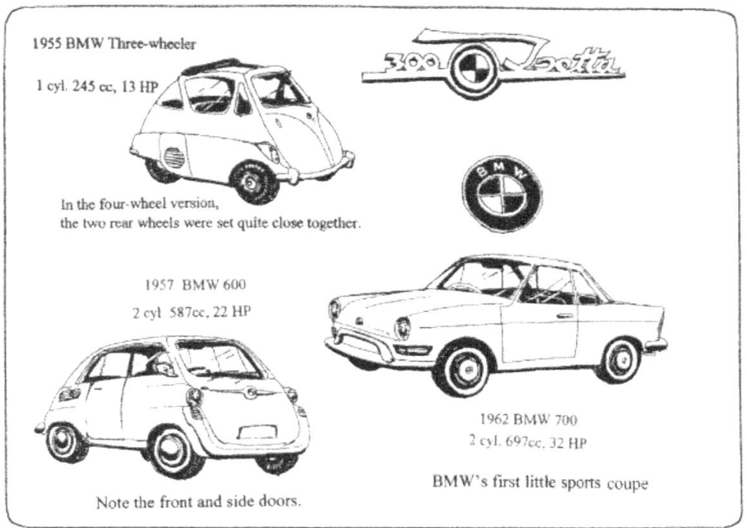

A couple years later, BMW came out with the 700. This handsome little car was just over 12 feet long but looked every bit as good as the rest of the company's stable of much larger cars. Its bodywork was by Michelotti, the famous Italian coachbuilder. Powered by a two-cylinder engine of 697cc, it was available both as a convertible and a deluxe coupe. An RS model was prepped and raced with much success, and soon, the legend of BMW sports coupes and sedans was born!

Now, let us take a break and look at some cars over the other side. You must have seen how Sinbad got around on his magic carpet. What if I told you that the Japanese had their Flying Feathers, and Auto Sandals too? Well, if you are in stitches now, wait till you see the list of all the wild cars they have in Japan on this Angelfire.com page. These names, though quite unreal, reportedly belonged to real cars: Nissan Big Thumb, Mazda Bongo Brawny, Mazda Familia Interplay, Toyota Active Vacation, Toyota Joy Canopy, Mitsubishi Mum 500—Shall We Join Us, Daihatsu—Bag 4, Suzuki Jimny—Wild Wind, Suzuki EV Joy Pop Sound.

The Seisakujo Flying Feather was Japan's Mr.Yukata Katayama's idea of a practical fuel-efficient car. He understood that weight was a big factor in fuel consumption, and so he specified light motorcycle-type tires for his creation. You might think that the man was crazy, but he was the engineer who was responsible for the racing successes of the Datsun B210. His racing "Bee" won the grueling Round Australia Rally in 1958 and boosted his career with Nissan. As the head of the company's, US operations, he was certainly not a flake. His minimalist car, powered by a V-twin of 350cc really moved, for the skinny tires on it had low rolling resistance. But, as it did look outlandish and awkward even while standing still, the idea never went big with Nissan. Thank God.

Another little car, the 1955 Fuji Cabin shown here was the joint effort of Isuzu, Hitachi Aviation and Fuji Automobile. The three-wheeler must have looked silly to the corporate "heavyweights" the day it was rolled out. Kind of roundish in shape, it was promptly dubbed a "boiled egg on wheels." It must have been no yoke to the two people who rode in it. They had to sit in a staggered manner, for the car was so cramped inside. Who would want it? But once we consider the little most of the people in Japan could afford at the time, and how narrow its smalltown roadways, we would appreciate the rhyme and reason for it. Although the Cabin was made specifically for sale in the Japanese homeland, a few of them got shipped stateside. One was recently discovered buried under a ton of trash in somebody's garage, quite ready to be "hatched," like so many old car restoration projects!

The Subaru 360 was imported here by entrepreneur extraordinaire, Malcolm Bricklin in 1968. The first mass-produced car built by Fuji Heavy Industries in 1958, it was powered by a two-cylinder, 20 HP engine, and was available also as a little truck and a mini van. Although great on gas, at over 66 MPG, it was considered a road hazard, being so small and light. Its odd body style got it nicknamed "The Jelly Mold Car." That did much to hurt sales, despite its low suggested retail of around $1200. At one time, some dealers even advertised cut-rate prices for those who would take them off their hands by the half-dozen. Be that as it may, the 360 did well in Asia and was in continuous production for over ten years. Remember back when we were checking out the German Lloyds? We talked about its boxer engines being used to power the first Subaru 360s. Now you know what humble beginnings this company came out of!

Through both the good and the bad years, Subaru pressed on, regardless, and learned to make what will sell here. It even got some ideas from Suzuki. The Justy, a rebadged Suzuki Swift was definitely a harbinger of good things to come for it had "on demand" four-wheel drive. An automatic using the transmatic system was also available for it. As Subaru forged ahead and proved its ability to compete, it made believers of us. In the year 2000, its cars were reportedly rolling out the dealerships at about 20 per hour—around the clock. Seven days a week. It was truly a remarkable turnaround!

Mitsubishi, another Japanese company, was already a well-established industrial leader by the forties. Established in 1917, it was part of Japan's largest industrial group prior to World War Two. Being heavily into shipbuilding, it adopted the stylized ship's propeller logo. Its motor-manufacturing division was not formed until 1970. Perhaps it was the 500 Super, Mitsubishi's first post-war car shown here, that helped this giant corporation set its focus on car-making. This little car offered the motoring public the most basic of transportation. It was a no-frills, bare-bones car powered by an air-cooled two-cylinder rear engine of 594cc capacity. It had a trunk, but whatever that needed to be stowed away had to be slid under the dash. Yet, this car had what it took for it was tough as nails. In the 1962

Malaysian Grand Prix in Macau, it swept the top four positions, winning the under 750cc class. As a result, sales of cars bearing the three-diamond logo sky-rocketed. The Colt line was started to take advantage of this boom, and it continues to this day, some forty plus years later.

Mitsubishi was instrumental in helping Hyundai of Korea and Proton of Malaysia break into automotive manufacturing in their respective countries. Over the years, these two upstart companies have grown from secondary assembly facilities, to full car-making enterprises. To give credit where credit is due, in the case of Hyundai, the contributions of British Leyland also have to be commended. The first all-Korean car, the Hyundai Pony debuted in 1975 with Mitsubishi power, Morris Marina body style, and Ford Cortina underpinnings.

Suzuki was first established in 1909 as the Suzuki Loom Works to serve the Japanese silk industry. Michio Suzuki, the founder, soon became famous for his precision machines. Although he was focused on building the best looms, he knew he had to diversify in order to keep the company solvent, for times were hard. The war years brought many changes and so, he branched out into making motorized bicycles. His bikes were so popular. Being that they were very innovative, it resulted in the government giving him a grant to continue doing R and D on them. Suzuki was soon in the forefront of bike making, with many full-sized motorcycles added to its line. In 1954, Michio Suzuki decided to change the company name to Suzuki Motor Corporation to better present its image. The following year, he introduced his first car—the Suzulight. This car was said to have started the mini-car age in Japan. The Frontes followed in the sixties, as did the Jimnys, its mini-jeeps. All were first manufactured with two-cylinder engines powering them.

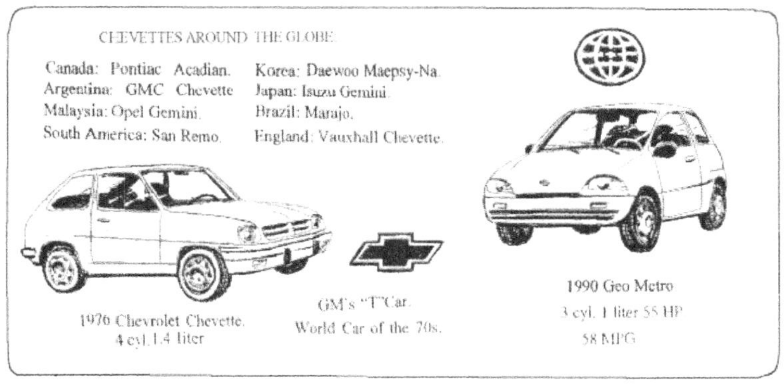

In the seventies, while the Suzuki motorcycle line was going from strength to strength, with many fine machines winning Grand Prix races and world championships everywhere, Suzuki cars were likewise performing excellently. 1985 was the first year American Suzuki Corporation started doing business stateside, and that year was its banner year with the cute and practical Samurai, a small offroader it introduced breaking all sales records.

In 1989, the Suzuki Swifts were getting the attention of more and more car buyers in the market for smaller fuel-efficient cars. GM saw where the trend was headed and soon entered into a deal with Suzuki where Swifts could be sold under the Geo nameplate as Metros. The General was looking for something new to carry on where its T-car—the Chevy Chevette had left off, and the Swift was "it." The Isuzu Impulse was also picked as its sporty companion and sold as the Geo Storm.

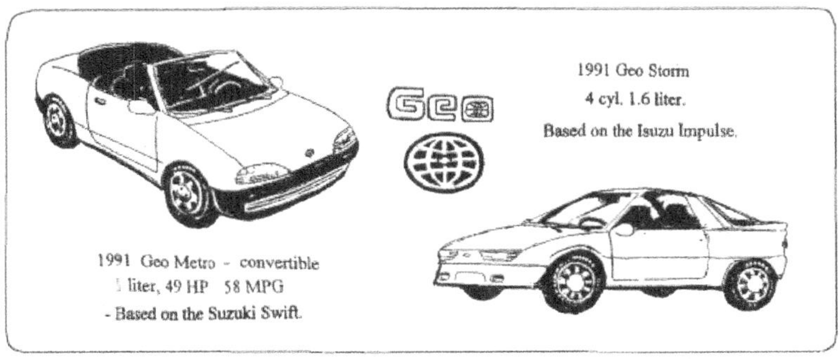

Mazda is another company that amazes me. Imagine a company that started as a cork factory in 1920 by one Jujiro Matsuda growing into what it is today. It all started when the company stepped out into machine tool manufacturing in 1929. By 1931, it had begun to roll out a line of small three-wheeled commercial trucks. With gasoline costing an arm and a leg in Japan, many businesses there had to make do with mopeds or motorized bicycles to help get things done. Mazda simply took an age-old idea and kicked it up a notch or two, and lo and behold, a powered utilitarian three-wheeled carry-all that will do the job twice as well at half the cost.

In 1960, it introduced its first mass-produced car, the R360, a two-seater micro, powered by a 356cc engine. This cute little coupe was just what many of those who needed a personal car to get about during those austere times had been wishing for. Over 20,000 of the 1961 models were sold. The larger (but not by much,) P600 came out the following year, and it too was a hit. A four-door micro-sedan that could seat four adults, it met the needs of those who wanted something small but with more usable room inside. It was not surprising then, that within three years, over a million R360s and P600s had been snapped up by happy customers.

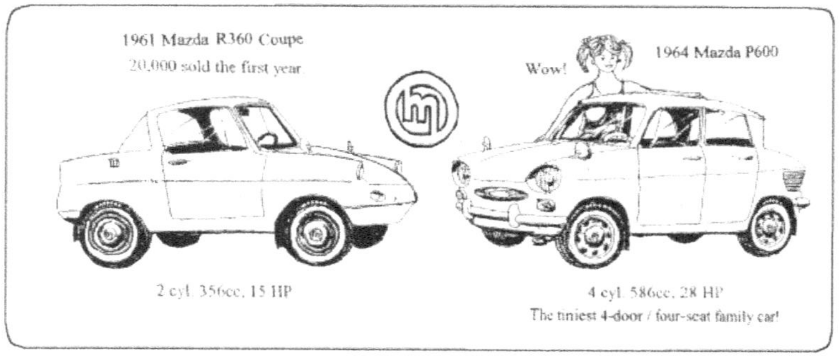

So, once again, we have proof that there is plenty of room for the smaller cars in any market segment. Today, with the price of gas going up and up, there must be untold millions who want a well-built, little car that will go the distance without having to be hooked up to the refinery. Just the hundreds of thousands living in the city alone, electing to go with a smaller car would reduce our need for foreign oil substantially. Just do the simple, straightforward math. Replace one gas-guzzler with one micro-gas-sipper and gas use would easily be cut by at least a fourth, if not a third.

Take a look again at the P600—the Mazda Carol. Consider its ingenious ultra-compact design. Check out how well the reverse-rake of its back-light fits in the case of this car. I take my hat off to its body stylist. He knows how to bend the rules without breaking them. The Carol, just 9.7 feet long, and powered by a 586cc, 28 HP engine, was truly a car for those who wanted the most car for the least amount of money.

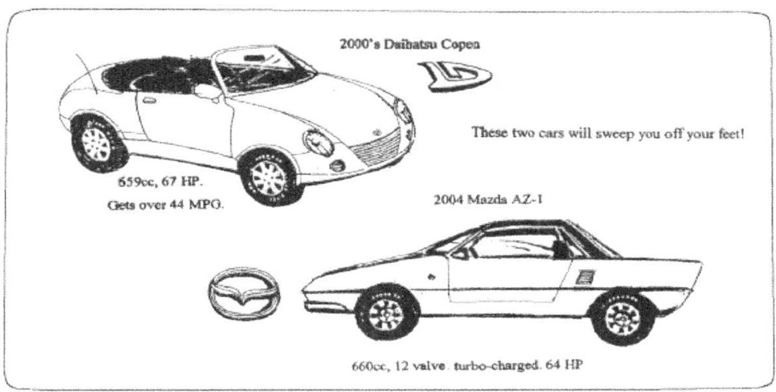

Mazda's latest hat trick has to be its super wedge-shaped micro-coupe, the Autozam AZ-1. Here again, we have a car that offers the max for the minimum. To say that this car comes loaded is an understatement. A turbo-charged 660cc, 12 valve engine drives this super sexy two-seater that sits so low you can touch the pavement from the driver's seat when the gull-wing door is up.

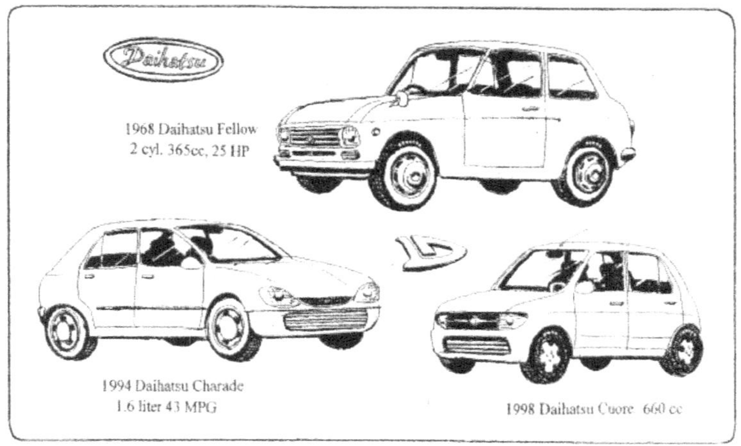

The Daihatsus would certainly fit well into this super-mini and micro category. Relatively unheard of here in the US, it made a big name for itself in England when it won the Round Britain Economy Run in 1991. This 3,621-mile rally put its 1987 Charade in the Guinness Book of World Records for it went 103.1 mile for a gallon of gas. That is a whopping 40 MPG better than most hybrids on the road today. So, once again, who needs to go hybrid for great gas mileage? Daihatsu also won the coveted "Green Apple Award" for showing itself to be a company that is environmentally responsible. Today it is partnered with Toyota and the First Auto Works of Red China to bring out the next generation of gas misers.

Quite a big player now in Europe with its Cuore, Sirion, Young RV, Copen and Terios lines, Daihatsu has forged ahead to work with AvtoVAZ (Volzhsky Automobilny Zavod) of Russia.

Toyota, like Suzuki was in the weaving business once upon a time. Established in 1937 by Sakichi Toyoda as "Toyoda Automatic Loom Works," the company grew within a few short years to become one of the world's leading manufacturers of weaving machines. By 1947, it had branched out into automobile production, and the rest, as they say again, is history.

As of this writing, Toyota, No.1 in Japan, is the third largest carmaker in the world and fast catching up to GM. It produces over 5.5 million vehicles per year. Quite a record, consider how shaky things were for the company in 1957, when it imported its first car, the Toyopet here. Those were the days when no one thought much of anything that came out of the Land of the Rising Sun. The stamp "Made in Japan" was looked upon with contempt by many, and most everything the Japanese made was the subject of much ridicule. How things have turned! Today, the Toyota nameplate is well-respected throughout the world. The Corolla, a mini-compact it imported to the US beginning in 1961 is now in its ninth generation and is presently made in Canada. For that this car line deserves a mention. Its Starlets, Paseos and Tercels were all gas mileage champs and sold well, based on Toyota's solid gold reputation for dependable cars. And when the company is worth over ten times more than General Motor's, that says a lot.

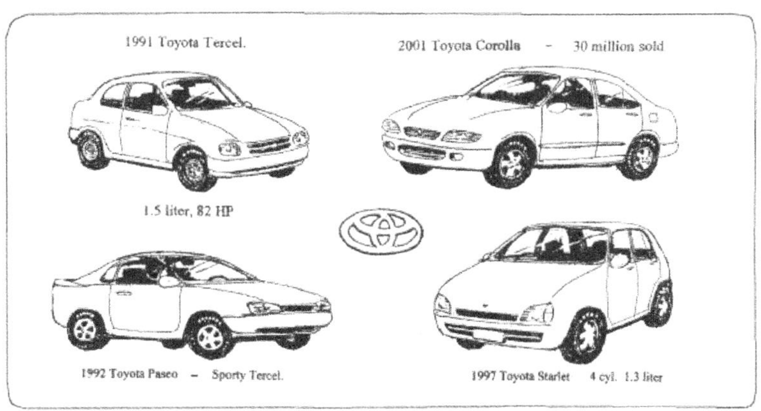

Featured in our show are the Toyota Publica 700 and the 800 of the sixties. They were practical people-cars, powered by two-cylinder engines. Even the superbly designed little 800 Sports had a twin of 790cc, tuned to put out 49 HP.

Like Toyota, Honda too, came from humble beginnings. Soichiro Honda's indomitable spirit was what got it going. The year was 1946, and Japan was just getting started to pull itself out of the rubble of the Pacific War. Most people could not afford much then.

Fuel was especially in short supply. So, Honda decided to salvage what was left of his machine shop and gear up to bring out the most economical mode of transportation possible, to help get the country rolling once again. He and his team started work by putting little gas engines on bicycles in a wooden shack which he called his "Research" facility. Well, we know the rest of it. From simple Honda mopeds to super-bikes; from humble CVCC Civics to hot VTECs, superb road and track records attest to this small company's rise to greatness.

When I was first shown the S600 sports car, I was utterly smitten by it. This is one fine machine! Quoting from "Hot Cars" it was "astonishing to behold." Put together like a precision watch, this tiny car had it all. It spoke so eloquently of Honda's technical prowess. The engine alone showcased its engineering expertise. Let me share with you this little write-up about the S800. Basically, the same as the S600, this sportster had a slightly larger engine which for its day was described by "Hot Cars" as astoundingly advanced. The engine was "a development of a light van engine with many motorcycle influences. The block is entirely cast aluminum, and it has twin overhead camshafts. It also features a single carburetor for each of the four cylinders and a roller-bearing crankshaft. Although the engine has a capacity of less than 800cc, it develops 781 BHP at a screaming 8,000 rpm—higher than most cars of the time. Despite its very high-revving nature, the engine is remarkably reliable." Indeed, all of Honda's skill in engine design must have been encapsulated within this amazing power plant. That Honda is recognized as the largest engine maker on this planet therefore comes at no surprise to me at all.

The first Honda imported into the US was the N360. The year was 1966. A mini-minimalist car, it was not what we would regard as something to drive then. The N600 too, which came soon after was sniffed at. Likewise, the Z600 "motorized shopping cart." That despite its great fuel mileage. But could it be that it was just a little ahead of its time?

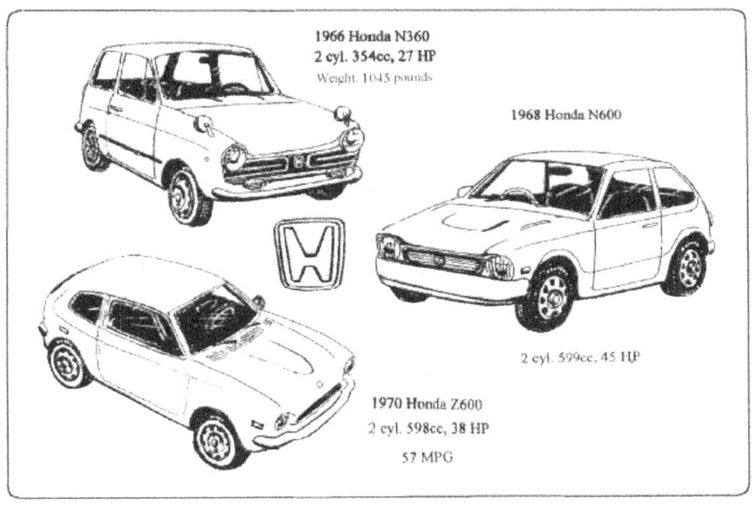

Well, look at the Civics now. (I still have my '96 Civic, by the way.) They are so awesome that they have become the perennial favorites of the tuner-boy-racer crowd. So also, the old CR-X del Sols, made in the early part of the nineties. Tipping the scales at 2300 pounds, this sporty mid-engine mini was no lightweight in both performance and gas mileage. It succeeded where the FIAT X1/9s and the Fieros failed. Honda should be proud. I am glad it kept working on its small car line even after the Z600s got the brush-off. It was because of its dedication to its R & D that brought us the revolutionary CVCC—its "miracle" ultralow emission, clean-burning vortex-controlled combustion chamber engine in 1975. Cars with that ingenious and yet simple technology did not need unleaded gas or the catalytic converter to meet the emissions requirements of that time. Amazing!

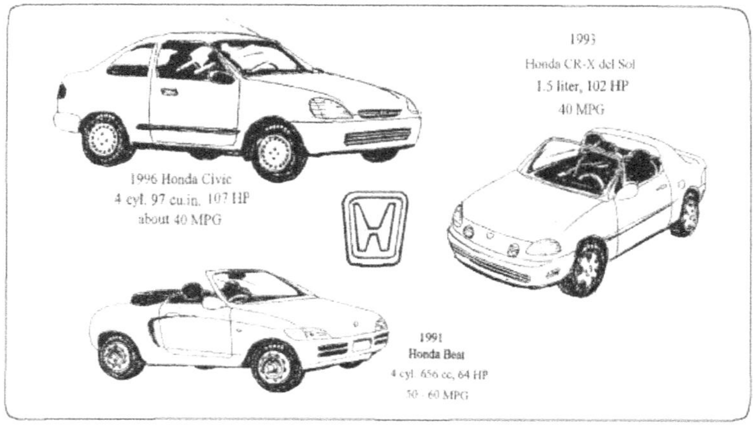

The Beat was one of the best Kei-cars when it came out in the early part of 1990. Even today, its rates a 10 on looks alone. Still much sought after here in the West, being fast and fun to drive, it is just now being imported by several companies in Canada. Check the Beat pages on the Web. Honda truly has its sights set on the future. As they say, "the beat goes on!"

So, who is to say that the smaller cars many not become popular again, in the not-too-distant future? Little personal cars or pickups, like our Guppy here. Made by Cony (which is now part of Nissan), this cute little "one-lunger" with room for two and say, a dozen sacks of goodies must have been one "helluva fine grocery-getter!" With an engine of just 199cc, you would not have to factor in the cost of gas even if you had to drive clear across town to chase down a bargain sale item.

Or maybe not. We have so many cars to choose from in this millennium. But you get the idea.

It is for this reason that I would like you to check out the Yugo. Here is one car that was the butt of many jokes. But do you know that it is in current production, and still going strong in Serbia-Montenegro (as of this writing)? This "reject" has its own fan club too, mind you, and all-Yugo car races are still the rage! Which goes to show that despite its poor standing in the Forbes' poll it can be as stellar a performer as any, in the right hands.

Imported from Yugoslavia in the eighties by Malcolm Bricklin, it got off to a good start. But alas, it was just not able to stand up to the "mash on the gas to go, stand on the brakes to stop" kind of driving we see everyday in Anytown, USA. So, will the new cars that our intrepid entrepreneur is planning to ship, this time from Chery of China, survive the daily floggings they are sure to get from the countless klutzy knuckleheads among us? That is the question.

The many makes and models shown in the next few pages should send a clear message to Detroit that the future belongs to the fuel-efficient. GM may be offering buyers of its gas hogs gas subsidies. But after the credits get used up, what then? So, is it not smarter for GM to just ease up on making the super large gas-guzzling vehicles? Instead of kidding around and humoring us with ridiculous come-ons, GM should get serious and buckle down to do what our European brethren are doing—building sensible cars for today.

CHAPTER FOUR

Modern Minis and Micros

As you can see, the cars in our show are already ages old. But it is to prove to you that our car makers had already the know-how to put out all the most fuel-efficient cars—years ago. Now, with today's latest high technology, should it not follow then, that they should be able to bring to us cars that are even more thrifty to run? We have seen so many cars of the fifties and sixties that were gas mileage champs of old earlier on in our show. If they reflected enlightened thinking on the part of engineers faced with a fuel crisis much like ours, what do our cars today say of our automakers?

With the price of gas at the pump ever headed upwards, should not Detroit be working overtime on a car that is able to squeeze every last mile out of a tankful of gas? Yet it seems that they are often going the exact opposite way. The rate they are pushing larger and more powerful cars and SUVs on the public, touting how good it is to live large must tell us that they do not have a handle on the current situation we are in. Or, could it be that our car-making moguls are just not mindful of the fact that they are losing out big time? What they are losing is also their credibility for so many of us now do see how they play their shell game of "size matters."

If you were in Europe today, you would be able to test drive cars like the FIAT Panda, Nissan Micra, Daihatsu Charade Range, the MCC Smart, Honda Fit, or the Toyota Yaris, and find each of them absolutely superb when it comes to gas mileage. The Panda gets almost 50 MPG. The Daihatsu does better, giving close to 70 MPG. No need to wait for the new Mitsubishi City Car, or the Subaru R1-e hybrid. There are many cars that have better than average gas mileage now to pick from. The Honda Fit points the way for it can be easily converted into a hydrogen fuel-cell car. Indeed, with Honda, working overtime on this new idea, it would not be too long before a practical hydrogen powered car will be imported here. But when that time comes, will it? Or will the deal somehow not fly because of Big Oil?

I bet the Big Three must have a hand in keeping the most fuel-efficient cars from coming to our shores. Take the Suzuki Alto. This car was first introduced in 1982. Improved year by year thereafter, it became the best minicar ever, by 1988. So, manufacturing facilities were set up in India to produce it as the Maruti as also in China under the ChangAn SC, the Jiangbei Alto, the Jiangnan JNJ Alto, and the Xian Alto nameplates. If this car was rebadged as the Chevy Alto and sold in Latin America, I wonder why was it not sold here too?

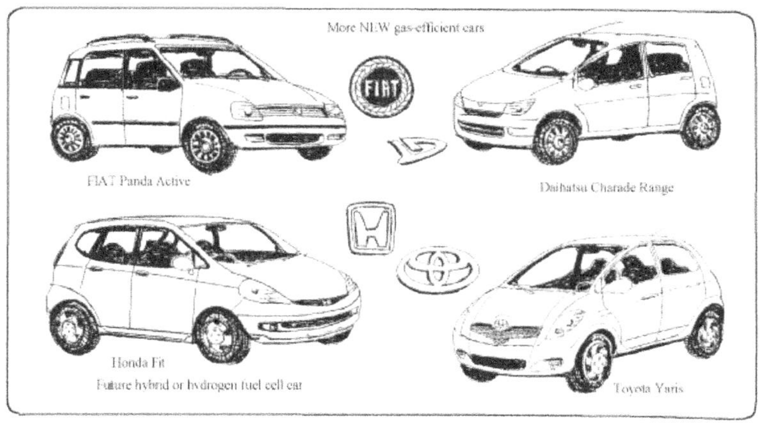

Well, if GM should fear these gas-sippers because they will make us see through all their gas credit shenanigans, they have a problem. They are not coming to grips with the fact that the day will soon be here when no amount of gas allowances will help those who buy into their bigger-than-life-is-better line. Or lie. People will simply tire of having to pay out so many of their hard-earned dollars just to feed their egos. A great number of people will be clamoring for cars like the super cute Suzuki Twin, once they see how suited to the times they are. These little cars that will be shown next are the new generation micro-cars I mentioned about on and off, all through this book. Small though they are, they will be big, when oil hits $100 a barrel, I guarantee you.

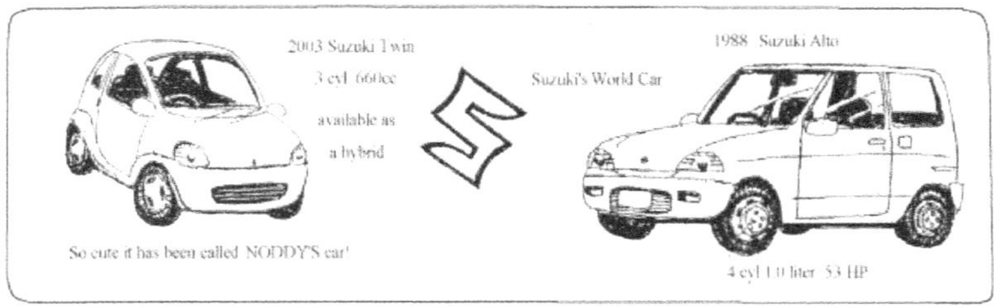

Remember the Virgo Range? This stylish micro can get over 62 miles per gallon. Made by Microcar SA in France, it has the wherewithal to revolutionize the urban motoring scene. Just 8.5 feet long and 4.5 feet wide, it would not be any problem for anyone to park it in the city. It is almost four feet shorter than the MINI.

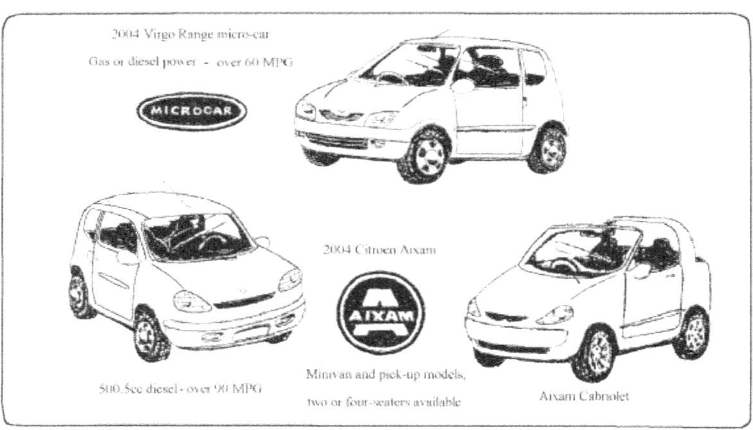

The Aixam, in production since 1975 is said to be the best-selling micro-car in Europe. Being a subsidiary of Citroen must be the reason why. Crash-tested, it is about the same size as the Virgo Range. As a matter of fact, most the micro-cars shown here are about 8 or 9 feet long. The Aixam gives around 90 MPG and can top 60 MPH. Like the Virgo Range, it costs around $11,000.

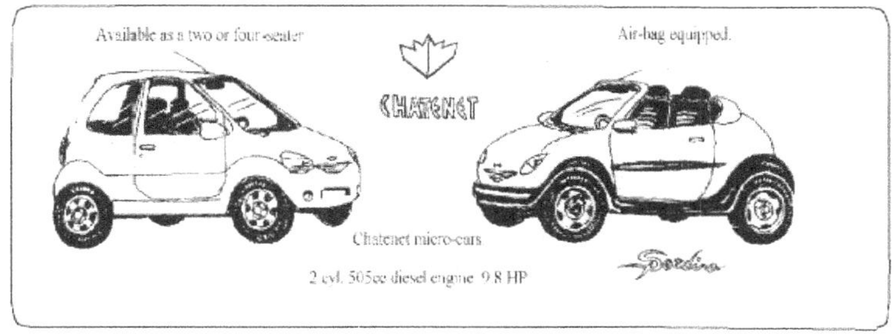

The Chatenet comes with airbags. For a tiny car, it is rather well equipped. Two versions are made—a sports model and a regular two-door coupe. Both are beautifully styled. The Speedino Sports looks like a winner. This topless is sexy! I could see many taking this to work, or down to the beach.

The Casalini, powered by a diesel engine of 500cc capacity, weighs just 770 pounds, and measures all of 8 feet long. Fuel mileage is excellent at 80 MPG. This micro-car is made in Italy. Being much safer than scooters, it has become popular with the teen crowd. Two too-cute models make up the Tasso line. Powered by a 505cc diesel, both the Hola and Bingo can go 80 miles for every gallon of fuel. The money you pocket driving them!

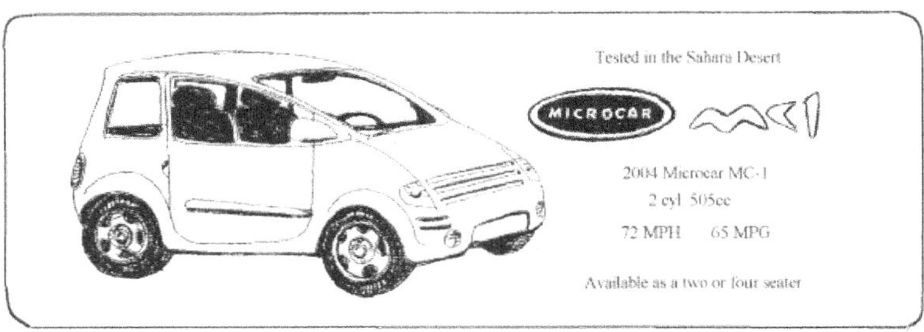

Microcar, the maker of Virgo Range also makes the MC-1. Go to microcar.com to find out more about this amazing car. It has been tested tough in the Sahara! Available as both a two and a four-seater, this micro is slightly larger at 9 feet long. Its 505cc engine, made by Lombardi/Renault has multi-point fuel-injection and produces 21 HP. The MC-1 has a top speed of 72 MPH and can travel over 65 miles for every gallon of gas. The car is manufactured in Nantes, France, and sells for about US $12,000.

The Ligier Ambra is an interesting micro in that it is built by a Formula One racing car company. Check out the old 1981 JS-4. You can plainly see that it was styled along the lines of little econoboxes of the period. The new Ambra, with a much smoother body can top 65 MPH and give over 85 miles per gallon. It has an automatic transmission that is like the Dutch Transmatic. Check the Ligier Ambra website and you will be treated to one of the best car brochures out there. You will not be disappointed.

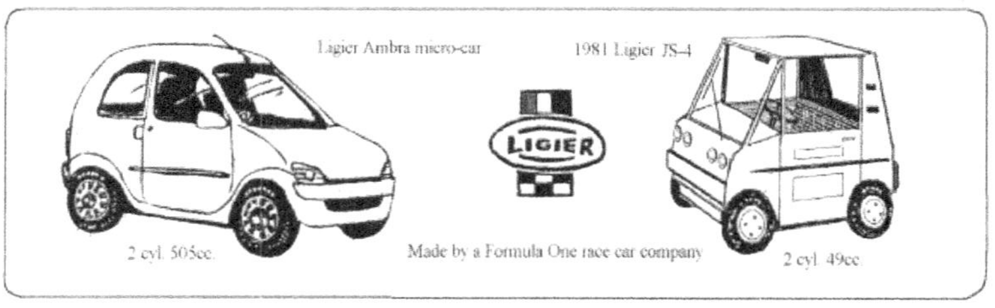

The current JDM micro is much like the current crop of micros although it is powered by a marine diesel.

The Canta, made in The Netherlands, however, is different in that it can be configured in any number of ways to suit the handicapped buyer. It is marvelous to see how well thought out this car is. There is a rear fold-down ramp for wheelchair access. With that option the passenger compartment would accommodate both wheelchair and occupant. What a pair of seven-league boots for the paraplegic, this little benchmark car!

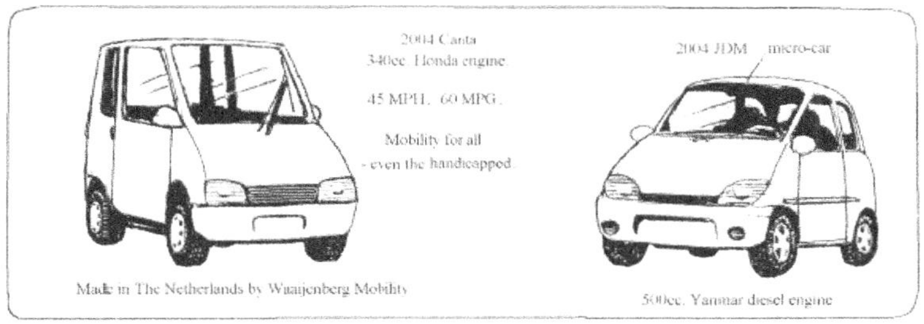

Imagine giving our disabled citizens the joy of once again being able to get around easily on their own. With so many new retirement communities designed and built to resemble little cities with interconnecting roadways linking all their facilities just for cars like the Canta, what's there not to like about these little get-abouts? Picture how liberating they can be!

One company, Unique, builds its cars to order. Two tiny models are available. One, the Q-Pod, looks very much like a sand-hopper. Its top speed is 45 MPH. The other, called the Q-T, is like a mini dune buggy. Both are street legal in Europe and the UK, believe it or not. The Q-T is under 8 feet long and weighs 877 pounds. It boasts a 5-speed transmission and gives over 60 MPG.

If the powers that be were to allow the importation and sales of cars like these stateside, I am sure many positive things would happen. I will just list three of them here. One, thousands upon thousands of new micro-car owners would be freed from the bother of having to constantly make sure there is enough gas in the tank just to get around. Without high monthly fuel bills to contend with anymore, many would lighten up and drive happier, and be more sharing of the road. Two, our carmakers would have to revise their stuck-in-the-mud "big is better" thinking as they too, come to understand the concept that small can be just as good. Seeing the ever-increasing numbers discover the joys of going micro, Detroit would have no choice but to retool to compete. Three, our nation would soon be weaned of its dependency on foreign oil. That alone will do wonders to help us in our war on terror. Consider the many subversive organizations that are being funded by our oil purchases.

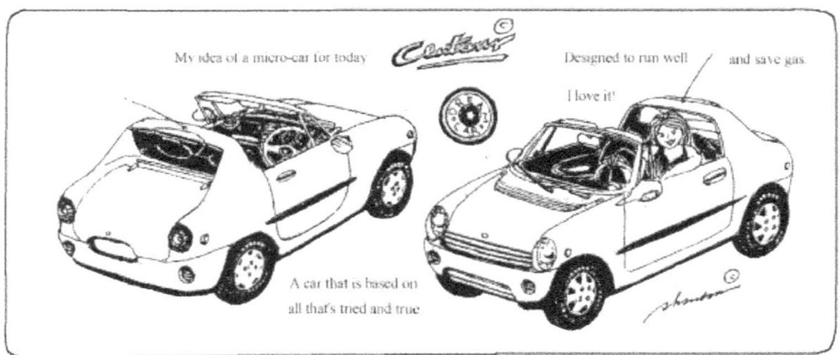

In closing, let me share with you a micro-dream car of my own design. About 10 feet long, my Centaur sits taller, and will be easy to get in and out of. Made with today's composite materials, it will weigh around 900 pounds, and yet be as solid as any car we have out on our roadways. As the body-shell is integral with the frame, all hinges can be externally mounted to simplify construction. This will cut production costs considerably. Built tough to run well, this back-to-basics car, is designed to be owner-maintained. Not loaded down with needless electronic gimmickry or any power-assisted nonsense, there will be little that will break on it. With a 500cc twin, it should be very economical to run. Imagine the dollars you will be putting back in your pocket, every time you drive it!

Organized by the Royal Motor Union of Liege in July 1958 for cars under 500cc, this rally ran non-stop from Liege in Belgium through Germany, Austria, Italy and Slovenia and back to Liege. Except for a break of a few hours in Brescia, 36 little cars bearing names like Zundapp, Lloyd, Vespa, Messerschmitt, Panhard, Goggomobil, Citroen, Isetta, and Frisky battled each other for 4 days over 2000 miles of highways, byways, switchbacks, and mountain passes.

Berkeleys led until the rally entered Slovenia when the FIATs took over and won the rally.

Call me a dreamer, but somehow, I am confident a whole line of cars like it would sooner than we know, be zipping about the landscape.

To thank you for bearing with me, I present to you, a dream three-wheeler along the lines of the Corbin Sparrow. Gas or electric, my "Rocket" has been configured as a two-seater.

Three-wheelers, like motorcycles, are fast and super economical to run. With them, you will not have to shell out $100 for a fill-up. Or to be heading to the gas station every other day, to fund some oil exec's billion-dollar-retirement just so you can get about. $15 would more than top one up and take you over 400 miles. The wads of cash a small capacity engine will save you will soon put so many smiles on your miles that you will be grinning from ear to ear. Never will you have to feed a black hole of a gas tank again. Instead you will be seeing your own wallet bust out at the seams with the money you will save—going micro.

You drive the carpool lanes too, in this zip-about. And you ride in comfort, for you will not have to eat bugs in the summertime, ever, or be forced to seek shelter under some overpass whenever it rains. Your CDs play in stereo within your own enclosed cabin boombox, with the one riding along cozying up close beside.

Well, there you have it. A mini and micro-car show of shows for you! I hope you have found it both fun and informative. Please feel free to comment on it. Send in your worst or best car votes with your reasons to: P.O.Box 4562, Timonium, MD 21094, USA. I welcome your input.

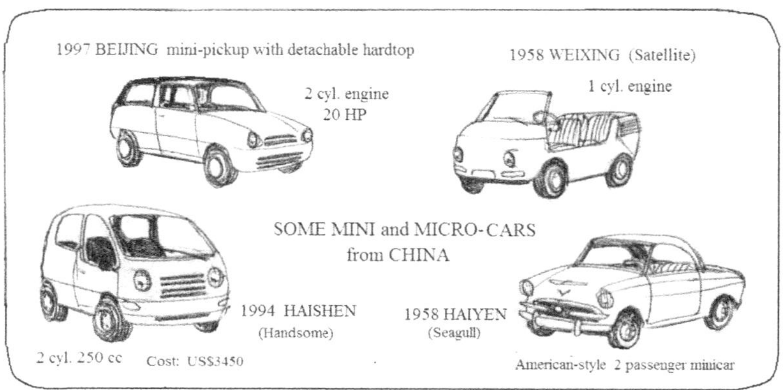

Tell me also what your favorite car is. I would like to compile a list and do a picture book of everybody's dream cars someday soon. Your write-up could be in it!

Look for future shows featuring cars currently produced in countries like China, India, Malaysia South America, and Africa. I have only touched on some of the more popular lines of this most practical class of cars. There are new mini and microcars being produced every year in both Europe and Asia. Recently, I read about retro-versions of the English Peels and the German Isettas. Talk about the popularity of these tiniest of cars! I hope to put together an album packed with cars that I believe are real beauties too, someday soon. So, stay in touch.

A final word: as the info within the covers of this show guide can be checked on the Internet, it would not be necessary for me to provide you with a long list of sources here. But I must credit these wonderful volumes, together with the countless issues of Dutch AutoWeek car magazines, for all the invaluable insights they have given me:

1. De Onschatbare Klassicker Jaarboek Nr.9 and 16.
2. Autodesign in Nederland by Jan Lammerse.
3. A Brooklands "Road Test" Limited Edition: Berkeley Sportscars.

And a million thanks too, to:
1. Mr. Henry J. Meadows for providing me with valuable information on his grandfather's delightful little car, the Frisky.
2. Mr. Erik van Ingen Schenau of the China Motor documentation Center for sending me his picture book of Chinese mini and micro-cars.
3. Mr. Terry Stuchlick of the NSU Enthusiasts Club and Mr. Stephen Boyd of the Scootacar Register for the fine material they sent to me.
4. Mr. Richard Campbell, Editor of Minutia, the magazine of The Microcar and Minicar Club for his favorable review of this book.

Made in the USA
Monee, IL
07 July 2026

56551631R00090